HORSES TO FOLLOW
2009/10 JUMPS SEASON

TIMEF☉RM

© **PORTWAY PRESS LIMITED 2009**

COPYRIGHT AND LIABILITY

Copyright in all Timeform Publications is strictly reserved by the Publishers and no material therein may be reproduced stored in a retrieval system or transmitted in any form or by any means electronic mechanical photocopying recording or otherwise without written permission of Portway Press Ltd.

Timeform Horses To Follow is published by Portway Press Ltd, Halifax, West Yorkshire HX1 1XF (Tel: 01422 330330 Fax: 01422 398017; e-mail: timeform@timeform.com). It is supplied to the purchaser for his personal use and on the understanding that its contents are not disclosed. Except where the purchaser is dealing as a consumer (as defined in the Unfair Contract Terms Act 1977 Section 12) all conditions warranties or terms relating to fitness for purpose merchantability or condition of the goods and whether implied by Statute Common Law or otherwise are excluded and no responsibility is accepted by the Publishers for any loss whatsoever caused by any acts errors or omissions whether negligent or otherwise of the Publishers their Servants Agents or otherwise.

ISBN 978 1 901570 75 5   Price £7.95

Printed and bound by the
Charlesworth Group,
Wakefield, UK 01924 204830

TIMEFORM
HORSES TO FOLLOW
2009/10 JUMPS SEASON

CONTENTS

FIFTY TO FOLLOW 2009/10	5
HORSES TO FOLLOW FROM IRELAND	45
THE BIG-NAME INTERVIEWS: PHILIP HOBBS, ALAN KING, DONALD McCAIN & TIM VAUGHAN	57
FUTURE STARS: REBECCA CURTIS, PAUL FLYNN, ANDY HAYNES, HARRY HAYNES, PETER TOOLE	77
HORSES OF INTEREST FROM THE SALES	85
TOTE 'TEN-TO-FOLLOW' COMPETITION	89
ANTE-POST BETTING	95
THE BIG RACES IN PERSPECTIVE	99
THE TIMEFORM 'TOP HUNDRED'	125
RACECOURSE CHARACTERISTICS	127

Timeform's Fifty To Follow

Timeform's Fifty To Follow, carefully chosen by members of Timeform's editorial staff, are listed below with their respective page numbers. A selection of ten (**marked in bold with a ★**) is made for those who prefer a smaller list.

Acordeon	5	Kangaroo Court	25
Alderley Rover	5	Lap of Honour	26
Alegralil ★	**6**	**Lie Forrit ★** 11/4	**27**
Andytown	7	Madame Mado	28
Atouchbetweenacara	8	**Marchand d'Argent ★**	**29**
Australia Day	9	Miss Overdrive	29
Bakbenscher	10	**Overrule ★**	**30**
Bensalem ★	**11**	Phoudamour	30
Carole's Legacy	12	Pliny	31
Carolina Lady	13	Qozak	32
Chilli Rose	14	**Qroktou ★**	**33**
Cockney Trucker	14	Qualypso d'Allier	34
Coin of The Realm	15	**Reve de Sivola ★**	**34**
Copper Bleu	15	Right Stuff	35
Cuckoo Pen	17	Ring Bo Ree	36
Dechiper	17	Somersby 7/2	37
Definity	18	Sona Sasta	37
Devon Native	19	Tara Taylor	38
Express Leader	20	Tasheba 8/1	38
Frascati Park ★	**21**	The Jigsaw Man	40
Garleton	22	Topjeu	40
Glenwood Knight ★	**22**	Touch of Irish	41
Harry The Hawk ★	**23**	Vamizi	42
Isn't That Lucky	24	Vino Griego	42
James de Vassy	24	Wymott	43

Timeform's Fifty To Follow 2009/10

Acordeon (Ire)　　　　　　　　　　　　　　h129p

5 b.g Accordion – Top Her Up (Ire) (Beneficial)
2008/9 F16g^2 F16s^5 F16s^2 16d* 20d^2 :: 2009/10 17s^{pu} May 15

As a half-brother to Having A Cut (winning pointer and third in Foxhunters at Aintree) from the family of useful staying chaser Tell The Nipper, it's almost certain that Acordeon's long-term future lies over fences, but he still has some mileage in him over the smaller obstacles and he shouldn't be long in adding to his sole career-success.

After showing plenty of promise in bumpers, Acordeon went off a warm order for a Ludlow maiden on his hurdling debut and duly delivered, beating Diamond Brook by two and three quarter lengths as the two pulled a long way clear of the rest. Although failing to add to that success in two subsequent attempts, Acordeon did suggest there'll be plenty more to come from him in the up-and-coming season. He was beaten sixteen lengths into second by Ogee in a novice at Uttoxeter on his next outing, form that looked a whole lot better when the winner went on to land the Sefton Novices' Hurdle at Aintree, while the fact Acordeon was pulled up on his handicap debut in May is not all it seems, having held every chance before blundering three out. Likely to prove best up to around two and a half miles, Acordeon has raced on good ground or softer.
N J Henderson

Trainer comment: "I think he ought to go chasing, but I think his mark is workable and he might win a hurdle first."

Alderley Rover (Ire)　　　　　　　　　　h106p F89

5 gr.g Beneficial – St Anne's Lady (Ire) (Roselier (Fr))
2008/9 F16d^3 16g^F 19g^F 16s^6 16s^3 17g^4 Mar 21

If there was a separate section to this publication which included those much sought after dark horses *Timeform* feel are potentially the furthest ahead of their handicap marks, then Alderley Rover would be one of the standouts on the list. The fact Alderley Rover boasts a hurdling record featuring two falls and only one placing hardly sounds a positive on that score, but he's far better than a quick glance at his form figures might suggest and such a profile should ensure he starts a much bigger price for his handicap debut than his ability warrants.

Alderley Rover was understandably given time to find his feet over hurdles after those early spills, but he was clearly getting the hang of things later in the season. He particularly caught the eye when fourth to a trio of fairly useful novices at Bangor on his final outing, left with plenty to do in relation to the principals yet halving the deficit from two out without being knocked about. Granted, there's a bit of guesswork involved in assessing what he'd have achieved there given a more positive ride, but it's safe to say he'd probably have finished in front of The Panama Kid and, with that in mind, a BHA mark of 111 looks lenient to say the least. An even more compelling case is made by his bumper form, the strength of which is there for all to see; he split Karabak and Merrydown at Market Rasen on his debut, and that pair ended their novice season rated 151 and 138 respectively. Alderley Rover is still a maiden, too, so connections always have the option of dipping back into novice company should they wish, but whatever route they take it seems sure we'll be seeing more like the real Alderley Rover in 2009/10. **D McCain Jnr**

Trainer comment: (See trainer interview, p71)

Alegralil ★   F109p

4 b.f King's Theatre (Ire) – Lucy Glitters (Ardross)
2008/9 F17g* :: 2009/10 F17d* May 16

Donald McCain might have taken over from his father only as recently as 2006, but the Cheshire trainer has already proved that he knows how to handle a promising young hurdler, having won the inaugural running of the David Nicholson Mares' Hurdle in 2008 with the novice Whiteoak. Although yet to jump a hurdle in public, Alegralil has shown enough in bumpers to suggest she'll be worth taking a similar path with in 2009/10.

Making her debut in a mares-only event at Market Rasen in April, Alegralil barely had to achieve fair form to make a winning start to her career, but promised better in how she travelled, also suggesting the experience would bring her on in edging left once shaken up to assert. Turned out in a similar contest six weeks later, Alegralil left that form well behind when readily accounting for a superior field at Bangor, the result never in doubt once she took over two furlongs out, full value for the eight-length margin over Cloudy Spirit.

Further to what she's shown on the track, Alegralil's pedigree also offers plenty with which to recommend her. As well as her as-yet unnamed full brother, who was recently purchased by Ginger McCain for €50,000, her dam Lucy Glitters, a winning hurdler/chaser during a light career, is a half-sister to the useful Sail By The Stars, a prolific staying chaser in 1997/8 who finished fifth in the 1998 Welsh

National. In addition, their dam Henry's True Love is a half-sister to the dam of top-class chaser Dublin Flyer. **D McCain Jnr**

Trainer comment: (See trainer interview, p71)

Andytown (Ire) h147 c99p
6 ch.g Old Vic – Pitfire (Ire) (Parliament)
2008/9 c20m⁴ 21s* 20s³ c20s⁴ 20d* 24d⁶ Apr 3

Nicky Henderson's record at the Cheltenham Festival stands out among current trainers, his tally of thirty-four attained since 1985 still nine ahead of next-best Paul Nicholls. In the all-time rankings, Henderson is second only to Fulke Walwyn, sharing that position with Martin Pipe. Ironically, it was victory in the inaugural Martin Pipe Conditional Jockeys' Handicap Hurdle with Andytown that drew Henderson alongside the fifteen-time champion trainer on that score.

Andytown first shot to prominence at Prestbury Park last November, winning another event for conditional jockeys rather comfortably from Maucaillou. Two disappointing runs followed, let down by his jumping in both a handicap

A Cheltenham Festival win for Andytown, who gets the better of outsider Midnight Chase (noseband)

hurdle at Wetherby and a muddling novice chase at Kempton. It was only then that Andytown built on his earlier promise back at Cheltenham in the Martin Pipe, scoring another ready success from a mark 18-lb higher than for his previous victory, beating Midnight Chase by nine lengths. Raised another 15 lb, Andytown seemed undone more by the trip than anything else stepped up to three miles at the Grand National meeting on what was his final start of the campaign. A well-made gelding, Irish point winner Andytown should prove equally proficient over fences as he is over hurdles and, with his yard's top-notch stable jockey Barry Geraghty yet to ride him over the larger obstacles, he should be making light of his chase mark—26 lb lower than his corresponding hurdle rating—in 2009/10. **N J Henderson**

Trainer comment: "We're concentrating on going back chasing as he's got 26 lb in hand. His jumping was disappointing, but he's spent a month schooling with eventer Karen Dixon."

Atouchbetweenacara (Ire)   h97+ c150p

8 b.g Lord Americo – Rosie Lil (Ire) (Roselier (Fr))
2008/9 c20d² c24g^F c24s² c21d* Apr 15

Tim Vaughan has excelled with horses from other yards, often bringing them out of the doldrums to string a sequence of wins together. In the main, he's had some pretty lowly material to work with, but that could hardly be any different in the case of Atouchbetweenacara, an already smart chaser who ended the 2008/9 season in the form of his life for Venetia Williams.

Atouchbetweenacara's chasing career was little over a year old when he landed his biggest prize to date, defying a mark of 129, some 28 lb higher than when making a successful chasing debut in March 2008, in the valuable Silver Trophy at Cheltenham in April, beating the reliable Private Be by twenty-four lengths with plenty in hand. A further rise in the weights clearly makes things more difficult, but there's nothing to suggest his progress has ended and he's sure to make his mark in some top handicaps this season before going on to even better things in graded company up to three miles.

Key with Atouchbetweenacara's improvement so far has been his attitude; he was bordering on headstrong in his early days, and Venetia Williams deserves credit for settling him and turning him into the likeable, enthusiastic type he is now. His jumping has become far more of an asset than a liability in recent runs as well, something that's also sure to continue to stand him in good stead. **T Vaughan**

Trainer comment: (See trainer interview, p73)

The bold Atouchbetweenacara looks an exciting recruit to Tim Vaughan's stable

Australia Day (Ire)   h131p

6 gr.g Key of Luck (USA) – Atalina (Fr) (Linamix (Fr))
2008/9 16g^2 :: 2009/10 16m* Sep 6 (Sep27F^2)

There are numerous examples of highly-rated horses from the Flat who have failed to make the grade as jumpers, Arc fourth Acropolis and listed-race winner Mountain a couple of the fairly recent ones, but we are confident that Australia Day won't be going the same way. Australia Day's form on the Flat isn't quite up to the standard set by the aforementioned duo, but it's bordering on smart and at Sandown in June he made all to win a handicap in good style (he also twice made the frame in good company during September).

Australia Day has had few opportunities to reach a similar level over hurdles, but given the way he is progressing it won't be long before he does. On his sole start last season, Australia Day split First Point (later won handicap at Cheltenham) and subsequent Swinton Hurdle winner Joe Jo Star at Ludlow: while, racing on ground firmer than good for the first time as a hurdler, he could hardly have been more impressive when landing the odds in a maiden at Worcester in September on his reappearance, making the running and still pulling for his head as he drew further clear in the straight. Australia Day is an exuberant front runner with plenty of speed and a fluent jumping technique, and the sharper the test the better for him over hurdles. He should be well worth following. **P R Webber**

Trainer comment: "He doesn't look too badly in off 113 does he? He'll probably go for a handicap at Kempton or somewhere like that, and, thanks to Jimmy Fortune who rode him on the Flat, we've now found out how best to ride him."

Bakbenscher h135p

6 gr.g Bob Back (USA) – Jessolle (Scallywag)
2008/9 16d* 16g 19s* 20g² Mar 7

We'd be happy enough with more of the same from Bakbenscher, who made a healthy contribution to the 2008/9 edition of this booklet with two wins from four starts, the second of those wins at odds of 11/2. Yet, truth be told, we'll be disappointed if he doesn't fare even better this time round, as he's now set to go chasing. Useful as he is over hurdles, it's over fences that the tall, good-topped Bakbenscher will really come into his own. It is also to be hoped that we see him in action a bit more often. Bakbenscher, brought along steadily, has made only seven appearances to date and has some way to go if he's to match his dam Jessolle on that score. Jessolle, who was fairly useful, ran thirty-five times, winning six races over hurdles and two over fences.

One of the best bumper horses in Britain in 2007/8, Bakbenscher landed the odds in a novice at Stratford on his hurdling debut but looked in need of further than two miles when disappointing on his next start. Stepped up to nineteen furlongs, Bakbescher regained the winning thread in a similar event at Newbury, where he beat Captain Americo by three lengths, and then showed further improvement tried at two and a half miles in the EBF Novices' Handicap Final at Sandown. Bakbenscher faced seventeen rivals at Sandown, in what was a strong field for this now well-established event, and he accounted for all but one of them. Jumping more fluently than previously, Bakbenscher travelled smoothly under a patient ride and made a promising-looking move in the straight, but he was unable to peg back Big Eared Fran. Bakbenscher, who has raced only on good ground or softer, is open to further improvement over hurdles, and he will certainly be of interest should he turn up in a handicap before tackling fences. **A King**

Trainer comment: (See trainer interview, p65)

Bensalem (Ire) ★   h146p F104

6 b.g Turtle Island (Ire) – Peace Time Girl (Ire) (Buckskin (Fr))
2008/9 F16s* 20d* 20d* 20v² 21s* Apr 17

Alan King saddled a Cheltenham Festival winner for the sixth successive year but, in truth, the 2009 meeting proved to be a rather frustrating one for the trainer, who had to endure plenty of near-misses (including with stable star Voy Por Ustedes) before Oh Crick gained that solitary success in the closing race. The disappointments weren't confined to the track, either, as the well-fancied Bensalem was ruled out of the Spa Novices' Hurdle at the beginning of Festival week due to scoping badly. That setback wasn't a serious one, however, as Bensalem proved when rounding off a highly satisfactory first season with victory in a much lower-profile novice back at Cheltenham in April, and the chances are he'll return there as a major player for the 2010 Festival, when the RSA Chase is likely to be on the agenda.

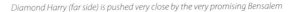

Diamond Harry (far side) is pushed very close by the very promising Bensalem

The gelding already has experience of larger obstacles, having easily landed a four-year-old maiden Irish point in late-2007 prior to joining present connections, and he certainly has the physique to suggest he'll come into his own over fences in 2009/10, whilst it should also be noted that there'll be few higher-rated hurdlers sent novice chasing this winter. Indeed, it was only a narrow defeat by the very smart Diamond Harry at Cheltenham in January which prevented a 100% record for Bensalem in 2008/9, a campaign that had begun with victory in a very hot bumper at Sandown in the autumn. Impressive novice hurdle wins at Chepstow and Leicester then preceded that close second at Cheltenham, where he pushed Diamond Harry all the way as they pulled well clear of some useful rivals. Both of those runs at Cheltenham came on very testing ground—connections sidestepped the Aintree Festival due to concerns about quicker conditions—and the chances are Bensalem will be suited by trips in excess of three miles in time, though it must be stressed that he's not short of speed. He's very much one to follow. **A King**

Trainer comment: (See trainer interview, p64)

Carole's Legacy   h135

5 ch.m Sir Harry Lewis (USA) – Carole's Crusader (Faustus (USA))
2008/9 16d^2 21s* 21s* 20d 21m^4 Mar 21

'She is the alpha female; a big, bustling, bad-tempered madam.' Such traits wouldn't usually be considered as 'Mother of the Year' material—even in a country which has twice awarded that title to Kerry Katona!—but this was the description that owner-breeder Paul Murphy has given to his eighteen-year-old broodmare Carole's Crusader, who won the equine equivalent of that maternal prize at the most recent Thoroughbred Breeders' Association Awards. Carole's Crusader had her share of temperament during her racing days (when a useful staying chaser for David Gandolfo), but Murphy is presumably happy to humour the mare's continuing mood swings given how successful she has been for him at stud, with her last three foals to reach the racecourse all tasting victory at least once in 2008/9.

Two of that trio, Mad Max and Carole's Legacy, are in training at Nicky Henderson's powerful Lambourn stable and both remain with plenty of potential for 2009/10 despite flopping at the latest Cheltenham Festival. Indeed, the mare Carole's Legacy may well return for another tilt at the David Nicholson Mares' Hurdle there next March, managing only eleventh in the 2009 renewal after her inexperience had rather got the better of her. The fact that Carole's Legacy was sent off at 12/1 fourth choice out of twenty-one runners illustrates how good a start she'd made over hurdles last winter, including wins in mares novices at Newbury (when beating the Cheltenham fourth Over Sixty) and Ludlow. A fine fourth place under top weight in the EBF Mares' Final back at Newbury on her final start suggests there could still be some untapped potential in her over hurdles, particularly once upped to three miles plus. However, Carole's Legacy makes even more appeal as a prospective chaser as, in common with her dam and siblings, she has bags of size about her and, in contrast to some of those relatives, she has looked a notably willing performer to date, too. **N J Henderson**

Trainer comment: "She could go hurdling or chasing. I've been looking after her at shorter trips and, if I thought she was good enough for the David Nicholson Mares' Race at Cheltenham, which she might be, we could leave chasing another year."

Carolina Lady (Ire) h103p

6 b.m Beneficial – Nanny Banks (Ire) (Fourstars Allstar (USA))
2008/9 16g^5 20d^2 Feb 17

John Spearing has gained a reputation as an astute placer of horses under both codes when presented with the right ammunition. The Worcester-based handler, a former amateur rider, has seen the likes of Run And Skip, Cree Bay, Thihn, Hakim and, most recently, the smart staying chaser Simon pass through his care during a career spanning nearly four decades. Thus it seems significant that Spearing forked out just shy of £20,000 for the twice-raced winning pointer Carolina Lady at the Doncaster May Sales in 2008. Based on a couple of runs in novice hurdles last season, the six-year-old looks like she'll have little problem recouping that purchase tag in the coming months. Carolina Lady was upped in trip at Southwell for her second start and shaped equally as well as the winner, Valleyofthedolls, having made smooth headway from further back. Furthermore, the horse they finished five lengths ahead of went on to oblige on her handicap debut before the close of the season. Given her pointing background, and the fact that her grandam was a fairly useful hurdler/chaser up to three miles, Carolina Lady seems sure to be suited by further than two and a half miles. **J L Spearing**

Trainer comment: "She's not ready yet. Handicaps will be her game and I think she's a stayer. She'll make a nice staying chaser in time."

Chilli Rose   F100

4 gr.f Classic Cliche (Ire) – Solo Rose (Roselier) (Fr)
2008/9 F16g* F17d⁶ Apr 3

Low-key meetings at Southwell rarely produce big-race pointers, though bumper wins at the course on the same card in March for the Alan King-trained pair of Chilli Rose and Miss Overdrive certainly caught the eye. Chilli Rose herself made a promising start to her career when landing the odds in a mares event, travelling strongly under a hold-up ride and staying on gamely to win by one and a half lengths from Seraglio. She was unable to follow-up in a listed event at Aintree, but did show marked improvement in finishing sixth of twenty to Candy Creek, better than the bare result, too, as she hung right from halfway and ran wide on the final bend. Considering that Chilli Rose is a half-sister to useful three-mile chaser Ross River and is bred to come into her own when tackling a stiffer test over jumps, the fact she showed a fairly useful level of form in two starts in bumpers is particularly encouraging. It will be very surprising if plenty of success doesn't come the way of Chilli Rose in mares novice hurdles in the coming months, particularly when she's tried over further. ***A King***

Trainer comment: (See trainer interview, p65)

Cockney Trucker (Ire)   127+

7 b.g Presenting – Kiltiernan Easter (Ire) (Broken Hearted)
2008/9 16g³ 16s* 19s⁵ 17d³ :: 2009/10 16g May 9

Useful novice hurdler Cockney Trucker already features in the ante-post market on Betfair for next year's Arkle, and there's no doubt that this lengthy half-brother to a winning pointer is a cracking novice chase prospect for 2009/10. However, he has a good handicap in him if persevered with over hurdles, as his runs in both the County and the Swinton in the spring demonstrate. With just three novice runs under his belt, Cockney Trucker acquitted himself particularly well in the former contest at Cheltenham, racing much more prominently than the others in the frame as he chased home American Trilogy. The test seemed sharper than ideal for him when finishing mid-division behind Joe Jo Star at Haydock two months later, and further improvement could be on the cards at two and a half miles and beyond, from a still lenient-looking BHA mark of 130. Cockney Trucker, who has raced on good ground or softer so far, looks one to follow in 2009/10 regardless of which route connections decide to take with him. ***P J Hobbs***

Trainer comment: "I'm confident he'll be a better horse over fences. He's still inexperienced even though he's seven, and we might consider a handicap hurdle first off."

Coin of The Realm (Ire)   h115+
4 b.g Galileo (Ire) – Common Knowledge (Rainbow Quest (USA))
2008/9 16g :: 2009/10 16s^2 May 15 (Aug19F)

Gary Moore is arguably the most successful dual purpose trainer currently operating in Britain, with a string of around a hundred horses, many of whom mix jumping and Flat racing with distinction. Take Wingman, Wyeth or, further back, Adopted Hero as examples, and Coin of The Realm very much fits the remit for 2009/10.

Coin of the Realm looks a certainly to win a maiden at the very least based on the promise he's shown in a couple of novice hurdles so far, splitting above-average pair Thumbs Up and Shiwawa at Aintree on the second occasion despite jumping as if the experience was still needed, which is just the sort of thing Moore will ensure is ironed out sooner rather than later. Moore's runners are rarely far away when the money is down, and the weight of support for Coin of The Realm at the Merseyside course spoke volumes on its own.

Losses are almost certainly merely lent, however, and Coin of The Realm's Flat form provides even more evidence to suggest that is indeed the case. After all, on just his second start on the level for Moore, having previously been with Ed Dunlop, Coin of The Realm improved still further to win a well-contested handicap at Epsom in June, showing himself a useful performer and, once more, not going unbacked as he did so.

Coin of The Realm stays a mile and a half well on the Flat, so further than two miles is unlikely to pose too many problems over jumps, and he'll be one for good handicaps later on after the formality of that first hurdling success. **G L Moore**

Trainer comment: "I think he's got quite a bright future. We'll break his maiden, see what mark he gets and take it from there."

Copper Bleu (Ire)   h145
7 b.g Pistolet Bleu (Ire) – Copper Supreme (Ire) (Supreme Leader)
2008/9 20s^3 16s* 16d^2 16d^4 20d^2 :: 2009/10 16s* May 1

Presenting Copper has proved a reliable handicapper for Philip Hobbs in both spheres of National Hunt racing but Copper Bleu, who was also bought out of Donal Coffey's stable, is already a class above his half-sister, having come

British raider Copper Bleu (left) is about to be left clear by Zaarito's last-flight fall

desperately close to Grade 2 success at Aintree on the penultimate outing of a highly progressive novice hurdling campaign.

The lightly-raced seven year old, who made the frame on all five starts (including in the Supreme Novices' Hurdle at Cheltenham) in 2008/9, rounded things off with success at the Punchestown Festival in May, winning cosily in the end after big threat Zaarito fell at the last. Smart though he is over hurdles, the chances are that Copper Bleu is going to make an even better chaser. A tall sort and already a winning pointer, he promises to take to fences very well and a prolific season in novice chases is fully expected. Copper Bleu has raced almost exclusively on going softer than good and needs a good test at two miles, so an end-of-season tilt at the Arkle is not out of the question, though he's sure to pick up his fair share of decent prizes before then. **P J Hobbs**

Trainer comment: "He'll go novice chasing. He's got the pace for two miles, but he'll stay further, and I think he could be one of the top novices this season."

Cuckoo Pen   F95
5 b.g Alflora (Ire) – Plaid Maid (Ire) (Executive Perk)
2008/9 F16s F17m^5 :: 2009/10 F16s^2 May 16

Plaid Maid showed herself a tremendously tough and useful staying handicap chaser around the turn of the century for her owner Lord Oaksey and his son-in-law trainer Mark Bradstock. However, it looks as if her racing days, which incorporated five wins from her final dozen starts, are going to be superseded by her accomplishments as a broodmare. Her first foal was Carruthers, by Kayf Tara, and he didn't take long to make an impact over hurdles before developing into a smart front-running novice chaser in 2008/9, exhibiting all the determination of his mother in the way he went about things.

In 2003 Plaid Maid was covered by Alflora and the resultant foal would be named Cuckoo Pen, after a field at the Oakseys' Wiltshire home. Cuckoo Pen's career hasn't progressed as far as the year-older Carruthers' had at the same stage, having raced in just three bumpers, but there has been ample promise in each of those outings and he very much appeals as the sort to make his mark in novice hurdles as his stamina is drawn out. The best of those three runs came most recently, when runner-up to No Principles at Uttoxeter in May, and it was encouraging to see Cuckoo Pen displaying some of the family's likeable traits, making most and battling well. Sadly, Plaid Maid died after giving birth to another foal to Kayf Tara just a few days after Carruthers had finished an honourable fourth in the RSA Chase at Cheltenham in March, but her legacy will surely live on. Besides Carruthers, Cuckoo Pen and the Kayf Tara foal, she is also responsible for the as-yet-unraced Carstaires (by Classic Cliche), a valuable 2008 filly by Overbury and a 2-y-o by Karinga Bay, who is already causing Bradstock to look to the future with great excitement. **M Bradstock**

Trainer comment: "He's a very, very, very nice horse. He had a wind operation over the summer and he'll go staying hurdling. He's a totally different horse to Carruthers. He's a much bigger, leaner, even weaker horse at the moment."

Dechiper (Ire)   h70p
7 b.g Almutawakel – Safiya (USA) (Riverman (USA))
2008/9 16g 16d 20m Nov 28 :: 2009/10 NR (Sep6F)

Finishes of eleventh, fifteenth and ninth, beaten a combined distance of one hundred and ninety-seven lengths and seemingly showing little aptitude for hurdling in two novice events and a maiden at the back end of 2008 may not be the usual profile of a hurdler to follow. However, Dechiper appeared to be set plenty to do and was never placed to challenge on all three starts, and since then he has enjoyed a fruitful Flat campaign, winning twice in handicaps at Newcastle during the summer. Therefore, we fully expect Dechiper to make a much better fist of things when returned to hurdling, especially as he's sure to be operating from a lowly mark. If translating some of his Flat ability to hurdling this time around, then he can hardly fail to pick up some low-grade handicaps. Dechiper's trainer has enjoyed a good start to the current National Hunt season, winning six races at the time of writing and looking all set to better his career-best tally of fifteen winners achieved in 2006/7. **R Johnson**

Trainer comment: "I think he's stronger this season and he's schooled fine. Two miles will be his trip and he goes on any ground."

Definity (Ire) h145+

6 b.g Definite Article – Ebony Jane (Roselier (Fr))
2008/9 22s* 24g* 24s² Apr 17

Graham Roach has enjoyed nearly as much success on the racecourse as he has in his professional career. The sixty-year-old, worth £75,000,000 according to the 2009 Sunday Times Rich List, is vice chairman of Tulip Ltd, the largest producer of

The well-bred Definity could go a long way over fences in 2009/10

pork in the UK, and picked up this year's Meat Management Excellence Award. However, the magnate will be better known in racing circles as the owner associated with the likes of Viking Flagship, Thisthatandtother, St Pirran and Shotgun Willy, and he looks to have another horse to carry his famous red and white silks to further big-race success in 2009/10 in the shape of Definity. The son of Definite Article took well to hurdling last season, scoring in novices at Wincanton and Newbury on his first two starts. He went on to improve on that form by some way when pitched into a minor event at Cheltenham two months later. A slight mistake at the last handed the initiative back to Tazbar, but Definity rallied to close the deficit to three quarters of a length by the line, the pair pulling clear of Franchoek, Blazing Bailey and Hills of Aran. However, being out of an Irish Grand National winner and already a winning pointer, chasing was always going to be the rangy, useful-looking Definity's game and, all being well, we expect him to develop into a live contender for the RSA Chase next spring. Definity has proved his effectiveness at three miles already, and to date has raced solely on good and soft ground. *P F Nicholls*

Trainer comment: "He'll be novice chasing. He's really exciting and could go right to the top of the pile."

Devon Native (Ire)   h106p F90

6 ch.m Double Trigger (Ire) – My Native Girl (Ire) (Be My Native (USA))
2008/9 F16g F16g^6 F17m^{pu} :: 2009/10 F16s^2 20d^2 21g* Jun 9

Devon Native, who improved markedly on her final run in bumpers when second to Jenny's Gold in a mares event at Towcester, has made an encouraging start to her hurdling career and should go on progressing for some time to come. A promising second in a novice at Uttoxeter on her hurdling debut, Devon Native then made all in a mares maiden at Southwell, where she jumped and travelled with plenty of enthusiasm in scoring by six lengths from Starlight Air, who went on to boost the form when winning at Worcester in July. Connections have expressed a wish to send Devon Native chasing, but she has the potential to go on to better things over hurdles before then, especially when tackling further than twenty-one furlongs. *C J Down*

Trainer comment: "She's been improving all the time. She's had a summer break and we'll start hurdling with a view to going chasing later on. She wants a trip."

Express Leader

h109p F107

6 b.g Supreme Leader – Karawa (Karinga Bay)
2008/9 F16s* F16s² 19g² Jan 1

Irish racing suffered a double blow in the summer of 1986 when the reigning winners of the Cheltenham Gold Cup and Queen Mother Champion Chase, Dawn Run and Buck House, both died aged just eight. Buck House might have lost out to Dawn Run on all seven of their meetings—including a specially-staged match at the Punchestown Festival—but he was a top-notch performer in his own right who would have taken a high rank in the two-mile chase division for several years to come had he not succumbed to colic whilst out at grass that summer. Express Leader is distantly related to Buck House—his grandam was an unraced half-sister to him—and the early signs suggest he hails from the best strand of this family since those days. Express Leader is one of just two foals out of the mare Karawa to reach the racecourse so far and both already look above-average prospects, with his year-younger half-sister Dare To Doubt winning two bumpers for Willie Mullins this summer. Express Leader tasted success in bumpers himself, shaping with abundant promise when winning at Wincanton in November (fellow Horse to Follow Acordeon was back in fifth) prior to finishing a good second to Shinrock Paddy in a listed event at Cheltenham.

On the strength of that bumper form, Express Leader was sent off 7/2-on favourite for a novice hurdle at Exeter on New Year's Day and, despite having to play second fiddle to 50/1-shot Manmoon, there was still plenty of encouragement to be gleaned from this hurdling debut. Indeed, Express Leader looked the likely winner until let down by mistakes at two of the final three flights, jumping errors which can probably be attributed to inexperience. He'll surely waste little time in going one better if kept to hurdles, but this rangy sort very much appeals as one who'll come into his own once sent chasing, particularly as he won the second of his two starts in maiden points for Richard Barber in 2008. Incidentally, Express Leader seems more of a stayer than Buck House and is likely to be suited by two and a half miles plus. ***P F Nicholls***

Trainer comment: "He'll run in one maiden hurdle and then go chasing. He's a staying chaser in the making and wants cut in the ground."

Frascati Park (Ire) ★ F117

5 b.g Bach (Ire) – Hot Curry (Ire) (Beau Sher)
2008/9 F17s* F16g² F17g* F16g* Mar 2

Frascati Park may have been missing from the line-ups for championship events at the Cheltenham, Aintree and Punchestown Festivals, but that shouldn't disguise the fact that he was one of the leading bumper performers of 2008/9. His Timeform rating of 117 was bettered by only five horses—all of whom contested at least one of those big races—and he appeals as an exciting novice hurdle prospect for 2009/10, when he'll have both a new trainer and jockey. In truth, his former trainer Carl Llewellyn will continue to have a hands-on role in the gelding's development, as Frascati Park is one of several horses to have followed Llewellyn in his move from Weathercock House stables in Lambourn (where he lost his job as salaried trainer this summer) to take up an assistant role at the Gloucestershire yard of former boss Nigel Twiston-Davies.

The change of jockey is likely to be far more significant, however, as owner-rider Barry Connell—who rides only in bumpers—most certainly lives up to his amateur status, with Frascati Park's third and final win of 2008/9 proving a case in point. The gelding had thirteen rivals for that run-of-the-mill contest at Stratford and was conceding weight all round under a double penalty for two bloodless wins at Market Rasen much earlier in the season, yet he had a far greater handicap to contend with than that. Admittedly, Frascati Park didn't help his partner by hanging right in the latter stages but Connell still had his limitations sorely exposed in becoming so unbalanced that he dropped both his whip and reins, leaving his mount to gallop home virtually unassisted in the straight and yet still claim a remarkable neck victory over Divy (who went on to win his next two starts). There is almost certainly bags of untapped potential to be gleaned from professional handling and he seems sure to make his mark over jumps, particularly as his half-brother Fix The Rib developed into a useful chaser in the latest campaign. **N A Twiston-Davies**

Assistant Trainer (Carl Llewellyn) comment: "We're very hopeful he'll go to the top. His bumper form worked out very well and he feels good at home. He may well start off at two miles, but we feel he'll be best over a trip."

Garleton (Ire)   h– c104
8 b.g Anshan – Another Grouse (Pragmatic)
2008/9 c25d³ c24m² c24v² c25s³ c27s c25g* c24d* c28m³ Apr 11

The decision of Berwick-based owner John Stephenson to switch his two National Hunt horses in training from the small Borders yard of Sandra Foster to that of Sue Smith paid dividends. Description went on to notch a hat-trick in handicap hurdles for his new yard, whilst Garleton also got his act together over obstacles. Sent off a warm order on the back of Description's transformation for his new connections, Garleton duly obliged at the first time of asking in a novice handicap at Catterick. He went on to make light work of a revised mark in a similar contest at Carlisle later in March, idling after running down the enterprisingly-ridden Indy Mood at the last. Garleton proved unable to emulate his stable-companion in a better race at Haydock, but he didn't jump anything like so fluently as he can, plugging on after crashing through the fourth last. A BHA mark of 99 still looks more than fair and further success can come the way of this strong-galloping type over the winter. **Mrs S J Smith**

Trainer comment: "He's a good fun horse who jumps particularly well. He's a three-mile handicap chaser and will definitely win races this season."

Glenwood Knight (Ire) ★   h116p F94+
6 ch.g Presenting – Glens Lady (Ire) (Mister Lord (USA))
2008/9 F16v² 17s² Dec 5

Ginger McCain isn't known as 'Mr Grand National' for nothing and, given his obsession with the Aintree showpiece, it is easy to see why he was attracted to this chestnut gelding when it came under the hammer as an unraced three-year-old—Glenwood Knight's dam is a half-sister to the 2000 National winner Papillon, who also finished fourth in the 2001 renewal and was placed twice in the Irish Grand National earlier in his career. It is far too early to say whether Glenwood Knight develops into a National horse himself, but he forms part of a sizeable group of promising youngsters currently housed at the Cheshire stables of Donald McCain, who has enjoyed three very successful seasons since taking over the licence from his colourful father.

Glenwood Knight has had only two starts to date, but both have promised better to come. A bumper at Hexham may not be the usual starting point for a good prospect, but one such contest there in early-November featured two of our *Horses to Follow*, with the debutant Glenwood Knight creating a good impression as he chased home previous winner Lie Forrit. Switched immediately to hurdles,

Glenwood Knight passed the post first in a novice at Exeter the following month, when he just got the better of a straight-long duel with Dastardly Dick. Unfortunately, the Exeter stewards took a dim view of Glenwood Knight's tendency to hang left on the run-in that day and, rather harshly, decided to reverse the placings of the first two. Whatever the merits of that controversial ruling, what isn't in question is that Glenwood Knight ran to a fairly useful level of form—he and Dastardly Dick pulled a long way clear of the remainder—and there is almost certainly better still to come too. Indeed, he seems a willing sort and should quickly gain compensation in a similar contest this winter. **D McCain Jnr**

Trainer comment: (See trainer interview, p71)

Harry The Hawk ★ h105+
5 b.g Pursuit of Love – Elora Gorge (Ire) (High Estate)
2008/9 16v^6 16d^5 16s 16s^5 Mar 3 :: 2009/10 NR (Sep4F)

In 2008/9, the Atlanta basketball team, the Hawks, enjoyed their first winning season for ten years. A victory over the Minnesota Timberwolves on March 23 secured it, much to the delight of their mascot, Harry The Hawk. They clinched a playoff berth for the second straight year, as well as earning home-court advantage for the first round of the play-offs against the Miami Heat, whom they defeated in seven games, before being swept aside by the Cleveland Cavaliers in the Eastern Conference semi-finals. The way the equine Harry The Hawk soared through his handicap debut over timber gives hope that he may himself attain a similar level of success in his field in 2009/10. In fact, Tim Walford's charge would have made a successful start in open company at Newcastle if he'd jumped more fluently. Ridden confidently in rear, he looked set to sweep by when a further mistake at the last cost him his momentum. That performance, allied with his form on the Flat over the summer (he showed himself to be better than ever when scoring at Doncaster towards the end of July) means that he could look thrown-in for his return from a mark only a pound higher than when last seen. Harry The Hawk has raced only on ground softer than good over hurdles, and is likely to prove best at a sharpish two miles for the time being. **T D Walford**

Trainer comment: "The plan is to go back jumping and he'll jump fences as well. He could be very well-in and he'll start off at two miles, though he may get two and a half."

Isn't That Lucky   h- c134p
6 b.g Alflora (Ire) – Blast Freeze (Ire) (Lafontaine (USA))
2008/9 c16m⁴ c17d² c16s⁴ c21d* c21d² c21m* Apr 11

'Lucky' isn't a tag which springs to mind if discussing Jonjo O'Neill's fortunes over the past few years. Although the trainer continues to saddle plenty of winners—he has topped a century in six of the last eight seasons—O'Neill has endured cruel luck with his leading big-race hopes over the same period. Stable stars Exotic Dancer and Wichita Lineman both died on the racecourse in 2008/9, Champion Hurdle hopeful Lingo was lost to a freak injury on the gallops, whilst top-class performers such as Black Jack Ketchum, Rhinestone Cowboy and Iris's Gift were all forced into premature retirement after suffering training problems. Isn't That Lucky has some way to go if he's to emulate the achievements of those names, but his staying-on second to Chapoturgeon in the Jewson Novices' Handicap Chase at the latest Cheltenham Festival suggests he'll be representing the stable in plenty more big races from now on.

Isn't That Lucky isn't the first member of his family to have contested the Jewson, as his useful half-brother Wee Robbie finished third in the 2007 renewal behind L'Antartique. The last-named gelding returned to Cheltenham the following autumn to win the Paddy Power Gold Cup, which appeals as an obvious autumn target for Isn't That Lucky, particularly as second-season chasers have an excellent record in it—Barbers Shop, for example, finished runner-up in both the Jewson and Paddy Power in 2008. Sound jumping was a feature of Isn't That Lucky's novice chase campaign, which included impressive wins at Stratford and Carlisle either side of that Cheltenham Festival appearance, and his profile has been a largely progressive one ever since his days in bumpers. Indeed, he seems sure to improve further once given the chance to tackle three miles plus, though that doesn't mean he'll be found wanting for speed if kept at around two and a half miles for the time being. A rangy gelding, he's a reliable sort and acts on soft and good to firm going. **Jonjo O'Neill**

Trainer comment: "He improved well last season and I like him. He should get into the Paddy Power Chase at the bottom, and may stay further later on."

James de Vassy (Fr)   h112p
4 b.g Lavirco (Ger) – Provenchere (Fr) (Son of Silver)
2008/9 16v* 16s 19s⁴ Feb 20

Nick Williams might have enjoyed plenty of success with horses he's recruited from other yards, including big-race winners such as Kings Brook and Maljimar, but the Devon-based trainer is now concentrating solely on young horses which 'no one has had the chance to muck up!', reasoning that 'the only horses that become stars are the ones you nurture from the start'. The four-year-old James de Vassy is one example of this policy and, although it is far too early to say whether he falls into the 'future star' category, the French-bred gelding appeals as one to follow in 2009/10, when a novice chase campaign could well reap dividends.

James de Vassy was a slow learner at home according to Williams, but he'd clearly been showing plenty on the gallops prior to his debut in a novice hurdle at Wincanton in late-January, when he overcame greenness to land a gamble (backed into 11/4 from 7/1) in quite impressive fashion. A tilt at one of the Aintree Festival novice hurdles was even mooted at that stage, but those plans were shelved following defeats on both subsequent starts. Admittedly that first reverse (when seventh of eight in a Sandown juvenile) was very disappointing in the light of his debut promise, but James de Vassy's fourth place in an above-average novice at Warwick on his final start was much more encouraging, particularly as he still looked green off the bridle in the latter stages. As a result, he seems sure to progress with further experience this winter, be it over hurdles or fences.
Nick Williams

Trainer comment: "I'm not going to run him until there's some cut in the ground. You'd hope there's some improvement to come from him—he's got scope."

Kangaroo Court (Ire)   h136 c122p

5 b.g Lahib (USA) – Tombazaan (Ire) (Good Thyne (USA))
2008/9 F16g 19g* 19d² 16d 19g* :: 2009/10 c16m* Sep 20

Possibly guilty of asking too much of the five-year-old on just his third outing over hurdles is the only crime for which Kangaroo Court's connections could be accused in 2008/9. Apart from that a sensibly patient policy was adopted with this promising five-year-old, one which looks sure to pay off handsomely in the long run.

Of course, the same connections could justifiably argue that Kangaroo Court was anything but overfaced when contesting the Supreme Novices' at Cheltenham given that another lightly-raced sort, Somersby, finished third in the race. On his previous start, when chasing home the smart Karabak at Ascot, Kangaroo Court had had Somersby one place and six lengths behind him. The deep-girthed Kangaroo Court, one of the nicest types in the field, was dropped in trip and failed to make much impression at Cheltenham. However, there was plenty to like about his performance at Ascot, and also when winning in ordinary novice company on his only other outings over hurdles, beating Honest John by

The useful Kangaroo Court promises to be at least as good over fences

seventeen lengths at Doncaster and Rear Gunner by six lengths at Lingfield. Kangaroo Court, who won a point in Ireland before joining his present yard, will stay beyond nineteen furlongs but had no problem kept to two miles when making a successful chasing debut at Uttoxeter recently. He appeals very much as the sort to go a long way in novice chases this season and another date at Cheltenham could beckon come March. **Miss E C Lavelle**

Trainer comment: "Everything is perfect with him and he'll continue novice chasing. He's a lot stronger and I think he'll make a better chaser than hurdler."

Lap of Honour (Ire) h103p

5 b.g Danehill Dancer (Ire) – Kingsridge (Ire) (King's Theatre (Ire))
2008/9 16s^{pu} 19d 16g^3 Apr 5

Connections of Lap of Honour haven't had cause to break into a celebratory jog since shelling out £10,000 to secure the gelding at the sales last autumn, but the chances are they could still have a bargain on their hands. Indeed, that sum is small fry compared to the 170,000 guineas paid for him as a yearling by high-profile owner Michael Tabor, in whose colours he won three times at around a mile in 2007 when trained by Neville Callaghan, showing form bordering on useful in the process. Lap of Honour proved much less consistent for Jennie Candlish in 2008 following another change of hands (for 75,000 guineas) but he did round off that otherwise disappointing Flat campaign with a victory at Newcastle on his final start before joining present connections. As that background might suggest, Lap of Honour is likely to need an emphasis on speed at around two miles to be seen to advantage over jumps and he never really encountered such conditions in three novice hurdles last season. Admittedly the ground was good for his final start at Hexham, but that testing track is hardly ideal for speedy types, so his eye-catching third to Best Lover there (when an unconsidered 40/1-shot) was particularly encouraging. Lap of Honour impressed greatly with the way he travelled through that race and also saw things out surprisingly well too, so he seems sure to build on that form once granted suitable conditions, with handicaps appealing as a good option for him. That certainly proved to be the case with his year-older half-brother Huguenot, who showed progressive form when switched to handicap company, winning once over hurdles and twice over fences in 2008/9 (all around two miles), developing into a fairly useful performer in the latter sphere. **Ferdy Murphy**

Trainer comment: "He's back in training. He took a while to find his feet, but he's had a summer break and has come back stronger. He should win a novice handicap or two."

Lie Forrit (Ire) ★   h125p F101

5 b.g Subtle Power (Ire) – Ben Roseler (Ire) (Beneficial)
2008/9 F16v* 20s² 20s* 21s* Feb 7

William Amos' generally modest string has allowed him only a handful of winners every year and he's often been heavily reliant on one or two. Reivers Moon and Extra Proud were his only source of winners up until 2006, but Lie Forrit already has shown himself a deal more talented than that pair and there should be plenty more to come from him.

Lie Forrit's impressive debut in 2007 was clearly unexpected, making a mockery of his 100/1 starting price to win a Carlisle bumper by seven lengths, and he started the 2008/9 season in similar fashion, beating Glenwood Knight at Hexham. Unsurprisingly stepped up in trip, Lie Forrit took to hurdling very well, immediately following up a most encouraging debut in a novice at Ayr by landing the odds in a similar event there. He made his handicap debut at the same course in February, on his final outing of the season, and showed further improvement as he made it four wins from just seven career starts, staying on strongly from an unpromising position to beat Thatlldoforme by one and a quarter lengths, again looking a thorough stayer. Lie Forrit goes well in the mud, and it's no coincidence that his only disappointing run to date took place away from testing conditions. He's one to keep on the right side, especially when his stamina is fully drawn out, still unexposed at three miles and beyond. ***W Amos***

Trainer comment: "He's come back a lot stronger. I've always thought he was a three-mile horse, and he's got a hell of a lot of guts."

Madame Mado (Fr)   F100
5 b.m Lost World (Ire) – Brume (Fr) (Courtroom (Fr))
2008/9 F17d^5 F16d* F16s^3 Nov 16

The ill-fated Le Volfoni was a good advert for the merit of buying precocious French-bred jumpers, as he packed an awful lot of racing into his all-too-brief career (he died aged just seven), running no less than thirty-six times over the course of less than four years. He proved notably durable after joining Paul Nicholls from France (where he made his debut over fences as a three-year-old), developing into a smart handicap chaser at up to three miles, twice making the frame in the Racing Post Chase at Kempton. The early signs suggest his half-sister Madame Mado has inherited plenty of that ability, but nothing like the same durability. The five-year-old mare has been restricted to just three bumper starts to date—Le Volfoni had run twenty-seven times at the same stage of his career—but hopefully this patient approach will reap dividends in 2009/10, when a novice hurdling campaign seems sure to bring about further success. Madame Mado showed progressive form in each of those bumper runs, winning a twenty-runner mares' event at Warwick in November on the second occasion, when she quickened five lengths clear of Santia (now a useful winning hurdler). Her third place to Shinrock Paddy and Express Leader (a fellow Horse to Follow) in a listed event at Cheltenham later that month was another creditable effort, particularly as she again impressed with the manner in which she travelled through the race. Madame Mado, like the diminutive Le Volfoni, may lack substance physically but that is unlikely to hold her back over jumps and trainer Nicky Henderson reports that she has already schooled well at home. There are plenty of opportunities for mares nowadays and she should have a good season over hurdles. ***N J Henderson***

Trainer comment: "She's a good mare, not the soundest but with plenty of talent. She jumps like a bird."

Marchand d'Argent (Fr) ★   h134+
6 b.h Marchand de Sable (USA) – Masslama (Fr) (No Pass No Sale)
2008/9 17d 17s⁶ 16s 17s* 16d³ 16g* Apr 4

Translating from the French, 'marchand d'argent' becomes 'money merchant' and it's to be hoped that the Phillip Hobbs-trained six-year-old of that name can turn plenty over during the course of the 2009/10 jumps campaign. A winning three-year-old in France, Marchand d'Argent kept ordinary company on the Flat for the most part (though once contested a Group 1 in the role of pacemaker), including being beaten in claimers. However, he looks like making much more of a name for himself over jumps. Switched to hurdling on his arrival in Britain, he caught the eye in a couple of novice events before routing the opposition on his handicap debut at Taunton, beating the subsequently-improved Picot de Say by an impressive eleven lengths. Although failing to capitalise on an excellent opportunity at Sandown next time in an amateur contest, Marchand d'Argent quickly put matters straight with another runaway success in a novice at Chepstow, this time by a ready six lengths from Oceana Gold, who went on to boost the form with some very solid efforts in handicaps. A fluent jumper and strong traveller, Marchand d'Argent isn't yet exposed entering into his second season over hurdles, and further success in handicaps around 2m should be forthcoming. ***P J Hobbs***

Trainer comment: "We've got several possibilities with him—he could go novice chasing, run back on the Flat or in a handicap hurdle from a mark of 125."

Miss Overdrive   F104
5 b.m Overbury (Ire) – Free Travel (Royalty)
2008/9 F16g* F17d⁵ Apr 3

Alan King has a good record with his horses in National Hunt Flat races—anyone shrewd enough to put £1 on every one of his runners in bumpers in the last five seasons would have shown a profit of almost £15, and Miss Overdrive contributed to that total on the first of her two starts in bumpers in the spring. That she should be so strong in the betting on her debut, when up against previous winner Hayes Princess and nine other fillies and mares in a bumper at Southwell, suggested that she had been showing plenty at home, and the five-year-old justified favouritism with a bit to spare. Miss Overdrive finished fifth to Candy Creek in a listed event at Aintree, one of twelve previous winners in the field, on her only other start, again showing signs of greenness but shaping as if she will have more to recommend her as a hurdler. In so doing, she went one place better than her sister, Over Sixty, in the same race twelve months earlier. Over Sixty has since made up into a useful hurdler who shapes as though she'll be suited by three miles. If she makes the same progress as her sister, Miss Overdrive is likely to have a bright future in mares novice hurdles. **A King**

Trainer comment: (See trainer interview, p65)

Overrule (USA) ★ h112P
5 b.g Diesis – Her Own Way (USA) (Danzig (USA))
2008/9 16g :: 2009/10 17g* Aug 22

An eight-length defeat of poor maiden hurdler Crosby Jemma in a weak novice hurdle at Market Rasen mightn't be the normal grounding for a member of the 'Fifty', but to say that that win is the only point in Overrule's favour is to do him a big disservice and he very much appeals as the sort to enhance trainer Brian Ellison's already healthy strike-rate over jumps. That's not to say Overrule's success at the Lincolnshire track wasn't without significance. Far from it, in fact, as by jumping and travelling fluently under a confident ride he went a very long way to showing he has what it takes to prove as good over hurdles as he was on the Flat, in which case he's sure to win plenty more races as a hurdler, and possibly some good ones. Whilst his Market Rasen win did serve a purpose, though, Flat form is indeed the key point where Overrule is concerned. His form in that sphere has gone to a new level this year, highlighted by his clear-cut win in a useful and competitive handicap at Carlisle over the summer, and it'll take some extremely punitive treatment from the handicapper to prevent him from making a smooth transition to handicap hurdles, even if getting qualified for such races requires Overrule to reach the frame in a novice in the interim, a race he's more likely than not to win. Stamina is another factor in Overrule's favour. He stays a mile and three quarters on the Flat, so trips in excess of two miles over hurdles are likely not only to prove within his compass, but enable him to progress as well. **B Ellison**

Trainer comment: "He's a very good horse who wants fast ground. He won easily the other day (at Market Rasen). He stays okay on the Flat and he'll stay two and a half miles over hurdles."

Phoudamour (Fr) h124 c108p
6 b.g Le Balafre (Fr) – Grande Folie (Fr) (Highlanders (Fr))
2008/9 20d³ 20s⁴ c23s^F 20s* 19d* Mar 8

One of the main reasons for the rise to prominence of French-bred horses in Britain has been their perceived precocity, as exemplified by the exploits of the likes of The Fellow, Gloria Victis, Voy Por Ustedes and Master Minded. Although Phoudamour may be French bred, his early education, which has included finishing runner-up in an Irish point and winning a bumper, is more typical of the traditional National Hunt horse, with the result that he's still learning his trade at the age of six. That being the case, we see the progressive Jonjo O'Neill-trained gelding as a promising prospect for the year ahead.

Phoumadour made a solid start to 2008/9 in two novice hurdles at Uttoxeter, fading into third after an eight-month break before being poorly placed when fourth just over two weeks later, future graded winners Cape Tribulation and Ogee filling the first two places in the latter. Phoudamour was then upped in trip for his chasing debut at Leicester, where he shaped like the best prospect, jumping fluently in the main and travelling strongly to three out before tiring badly and coming down at the last. Offered a short break, it was in his last two starts that Phoudamour started to fulfil earlier promise, beating subsequent dual-winner Pterodactyl at Hereford before scoring again at Market Rasen, seeming to idle as he beat Quentin Collonges, the pair a distance clear. Given a far from insurmountable mark and having the scope to do much better over fences in particular, Phoudamour looks likely to progress and win handicaps in the coming season. ***Jonjo O'Neill***

Trainer comment: "I thought he was really nice at first. He'll go back chasing, which may bring out the best in him."

Pliny (Ire)   h105p F100

5 b.g Accordion – American Chick (Ire) (Lord Americo)
2008/9 F16d⁵ F16s* 20s⁵ Feb 21

Gaius Plinius Caecilius Secundus, known as Pliny the Younger, was a lawyer, author, and magistrate of Ancient Rome. Brought up by his uncle, Pliny the Elder, they both witnessed the eruption of Vesuvius on 24th August 79 AD, an event which the younger famously documented to his friend, the historian Tacitus. Hopefully race readers will have much to recount about the feats of Pliny's equine namesake in 2009/10. The Marie Shone-owned gelding more than confirmed the promise of his debut when drawing clear from the furlong pole in a bumper at Towcester on Boxing Day. On the back of that, Pliny was sent off the most fancied of those making their hurdling debuts in a maiden at Chepstow two months later. He shaped as if likely to be suited by an even stiffer test of stamina, however, the steady pace proving a hindrance as he finished fifth behind Hey Big Spender. Pliny has so far raced only on good to soft/soft ground and looks the type to do well when his stamina is tested more fully over hurdles in the coming season, hopefully providing compensation of sorts for connections, who tragically lost their smart chaser Nil Desperandum a couple of years ago. **Miss Venetia Williams**

Trainer comment: "He's in training now and he'll be hurdling. He's going to be a stayer in due course. He's a young horse and hopefully there'll be natural improvement in him."

Qozak (Fr) h128p

5 b.g Apple Tree (Fr) – Good Girl (Fr) (Vorias (USA))
2008/9 F11d[5] F12d[2] F11g* F12s* F12d[3] 16s[2] 17s* 19s* 16d[4] Apr 4

The form of last season's John Smith's Handicap Hurdle at Aintree's Grand National meeting, a race confined to conditional jockeys and amateur riders for the first time, is working out well to say the least. Whilst the winner, Culcabock, subsequently flopped in the Scottish Chamipon Hurdle, the third- and fifth-placed horses, Joe Jo Star and Hot Diamond, went on to finish first and third respectively in the Swinton at Haydock in May. Awesome George and Mutual Friend finished further down the field but went on to win their next start, and Red Admiral, Seven Is My Number and I Have Dreamed subsequently made bright starts to their chasing careers. Nevertheless, the horse we predict has the

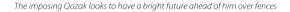

The imposing Qozak looks to have a bright future ahead of him over fences

brightest future of any of the twenty-one to compete hasn't been sighted since. A four-time bumper winner in his native France before being purchased by Messrs Barber and Findlay, Qozak had won a couple of novice hurdles on soft ground at Taunton before turning up at Aintree. He wasn't suited by the relative test of speed in what was an altogether more competitive contest and did well to finish fourth in the circumstances, just under five lengths behind Culcabock. Qozak remains open to improvement back over further and most likely has a similarly valuable handicap in him were he to be kept to timber. As a big gelding, however, it would be entirely understandable if connections looked to crack on with him over fences. ***P F Nicholls***

Trainer comment: "I think he could progress nicely. He's had a breathing operation and he'll go novice chasing."

Qroktou (Fr) ★   F116

5 b.g Fragrant Mix (Ire) – Cathou (Fr) (Quart de Vin (Fr))
2008/9 F16s F16d* F16m^2 Apr 13

There's a very good chance Qroktou's potential as a novice hurdler could go under the radar and he's well worth backing to confirm as much in 2009/10. Qroktou had three runs in bumpers at a relatively low-key level, avoiding any of the main festivals which draw so much attention, yet the standard of form he showed through that trio of starts would, in theory, have seen him dead heat for fourth in the Champion Bumper at Cheltenham in March. The one who Qroktou would have shared that position with was Quel Esprit, the first home of Willie Mullins' eight-strong Festival contingent, but in the unlikely event of the two pitching up in a novice hurdle together, then there's no doubt who the market would side with, possibly wrongly given how solid Qroktou's form appears. Admittedly, his debut at Sandown didn't obviously mark him down as a useful bumper performer, but Qroktou flourished in two runs thereafter, proving too strong for fifteen rivals in a well-run affair at Newbury before acquitting himself with great credit in failing by less than a length to concede 7 lb to the well-touted Paul Nicholls-trained debutant Aiteen Thirtythree at Chepstow, with fellow previous winner Double Pride fully eighteen lengths adrift in third. The time at Chepstow in relation to the second division of the bumper forty minutes later fully backs up the positive view taken of the form and, encouragingly with a view to jumping, Qroktou's runs have been characterised by a straightforward, enthusiastic nature. He's a good-looking type, too, as well as a half-brother to useful French chaser Ommega, and don't be as surprised as some might be if he makes his mark in top novice company this term. ***P J Hobbs***

Trainer comment: "He's very interesting and I'd be positive about him. He'll go straight over hurdles now and he'll want a stiff two miles at least."

Qualypso d'Allier (Fr)   h81 c91p
5 b.g Dark Moondancer – Miss Akarad (Fr) (Akarad (Fr))
2008/9 19s c16s c23d⁴ 23m⁵ Apr 14

'Never invest in anything that eats or needs repairing'. So said the late American impresario Billy Rose, whose sound piece of financial advice presumably never filtered through to big-spending owner Dr John Hollowood. The latter's ambitious plans in the late-nineties saw him purchase a couple of historic yards in Yorkshire (the first one for a reputed £1 million) for his trainer Andy Turnell, plus pay a then-record 200,000 guineas for Gatflax at the Doncaster October Sales in 1998, only to endure decidedly mixed results before selling up earlier this decade—Gatflax, for example, won just three times (recouping a mere £10,000) from thirty-three starts for Hollowood. That experience clearly hasn't deterred Turnell nor, more importantly, his current principal backer, Scottish businessman Mark Tedham, who has invested just as heavily at the sales in recent seasons. Tedham shelled out £300,000 on two horses at the Cheltenham April Sales in 2008 and both ran in his yellow and dark blue colours for Turnell in 2008/9. Micheal Flips made some inroads into his £200,000 price tag and was even considered good enough to run at the Cheltenham Festival, but Qualypso d'Allier has so far fallen into the 'costly flop' category, finishing last on both starts over fences and also down the field in two novice hurdles. That could be about to change in 2009/10, however, as the chances are we haven't seen anything like the best of Qualypso d'Allier yet under Rules, particularly as he'd looked an exciting prospect when a wide-margin winner of a maiden point prior to visiting the sale ring. A half-brother to the useful staying chaser Kandjar d'Allier, this five-year-old certainly looks the part and seems sure to benefit physically from another summer under his belt. He could be one to look out for in lowly handicap chases at around two and a half miles. **Andrew Turnell**

Trainer comment: "He'll go chasing again this season. He's strengthened up and looks a different horse now, and he could improve considerably."

Reve de Sivola (Fr) ★   h138
4 b.g Assessor (Ire) – Eva de Chalamont (Fr) (Iron Duke (Fr))
2008/9 16g⁶ 16s³ 16d³ 17v² 17d⁶ Mar 13

The Paul Duffy Diamond Partnership was fortunate enough to have two runners which carried its colours at the 2009 Cheltenham Festival, though the duo in question (both trained by Nick Williams) had vastly different profiles. Whereas stable star Diamond Harry had been unbeaten in four previous starts over hurdles (plus two lucrative bumper wins), the juvenile Reve de Sivola had drawn a blank from the same number of outings and was the only maiden in an eighteen-strong line-up for the Triumph Hurdle. It seems unlikely, however, that Reve de Sivola will remain a maiden for much longer and a second campaign over hurdles should reap dividends in 2009/10, particularly once stepped up in trip. Indeed, the Baring Bingham Novices' Hurdle (over two miles five furlongs) has already been mooted as the gelding's long-term target and, if things go to plan, he'll be bidding to go two places better than Diamond Harry did in the 2009 renewal. Reve de Sivola also finished in the money (just!) at the latest Festival, his sixth place in the Triumph (which earned connections £1,608) a creditable performance in amongst another above-average crop of juveniles, though it did rather expose his limitations when racing around the minimum trip. He'd shaped as if in need of further on most previous starts, including when placed behind the very smart Walkon in graded events at Chepstow and Cheltenham, usually doing all of his best work late on. Reve de Sivola's sire Assessor was a stayer on the Flat and has been an influence for stamina at stud, which gives further weight to the theory that improvement will be forthcoming once campaigned at two-and-a-half miles plus, whilst the fact this French-bred gelding didn't race on the Flat suggests that lack of experience might also have been a factor on occasions in 2008/9 (he was sometimes let down by his jumping). **Nick Williams**

Trainer comment: "He's scheduled to run first time out at Cheltenham on October 17. He's going to target the big novices, with the Sharp there in mid-November a later possibility. I'm not sure if he'll stay at two miles, but he'll certainly start over that trip."

Right Stuff (Fr) h115p

6 b.g Dansili – Specificity (USA) (Alleged (USA))
2008/9 16g^2 16m^3 17s^6 :: 2009/10 16m 16g^3 Jul 30 (Aug14F^2)

A fairly useful performer on the Flat, winning five times up to a mile and a half, Right Stuff is likely to prove at least as good over hurdles judged on the promise he's shown in five runs over timber for Gary Moore. Right Stuff was placed in two of his three starts in novice hurdles, his best effort when second to Shore Thing at Towcester on his hurdling debut in 2008/9. He started life in handicap hurdles in the current season off a mark more indicative of his Flat form, but looked to have running left in him when a creditable seventh at Stratford in May, only his jumping letting him down. Right Stuff's fluency again deserted him in a similar event at Stratford on his most recent start over hurdles, but overall he again shaped very well, moving into contention before a couple of blunders in the closing stages. Right Stuff produced his best effort yet on the Flat when second to Oasis Night over a mile and five furlongs at Newbury in August, and we fully expect him to step up on what he has shown over hurdles so far when he's given the opportunity to tackle two and a quarter miles and more, while his jumping should become more fluent as he gains further experience. **G L Moore**

Trainer comment: "He's been a bit disappointing, but I think I've been running him on the wrong tracks. His Flat form is very good and we'll wait for the bigger courses to start again now."

Ring Bo Ree (Ire) h102

6 b.g Topanoora – La Ronde (Common Grounds)
2008/9 21s^F 20g* 17d^2 21s^4 Feb 7

Ring Bo Ree had shown glimmers of promise in three maiden hurdles as a four-year-old and it was no surprise to see him shape as though about to do much better on his handicap/seasonal debut at Ludlow in November. A step up in trip was an obvious reason for him to be seen in a better light, but the way in which he travelled and made up ground was proof that he'd improved plenty regardless. Unfortunately, the Tom George-trained gelding fell at the last whilst holding every chance, but it didn't take him long to make up for it, going on to justify odds-on-favouritism at Hereford a week later.

Although that proved to be his only success of the season, Ring Bo Ree should add to his tally if his two subsequent outings are anything to go by. A couple of late mistakes meant that he could manage to finish only second at Cheltenham and then fourth at Kempton, where he matched the thrown-in Bally Conn for a long way. Ring Bo Ree travelled powerfully on both those occasions and is evidently still ahead of his mark over hurdles, while he also looks the sort who should go on and make his presence felt over fences. He stays twenty-one furlongs, and has raced only on good ground or softer. **T R George**

Trainer comment: "He was slightly late coming back in and probably won't run until near Christmas time. I envisage him going novice handicap chasing, which will hopefully be his forte."

Somersby (Ire) h141

5 b.g Second Empire (Ire) – Back To Roost (Ire) (Presenting)
2008/9 16d⁴ 16g* 19d³ 16d³ 16d³ Apr 3

That Somersby won only once last season doesn't represent anything like a fair reflection of the progress he made over hurdles, and this improving five-year-old can surely make amends for that lack of success over fences this time around. Successful on his only start in bumpers in 2007/08, Somersby got off the mark over timber at the second time of asking in a novice hurdle at Kempton, travelling strongly and not at all extended to assert in good style. Somersby stepped up markedly on that form when third behind Go Native and Medermit in the Supreme Novices' Hurdle at Cheltenham in March, and confirmed himself a smart novice when occupying the same position in a Grade 2 event won by El Dancer at Aintree in April. The undoubted ability and likeable attitude he demonstrated last season aren't the only reasons for thinking that Somersby will do very well over fences. He has a solid jumping pedigree—from the family of smart 2m/3m chaser Mr Baxter Basics—and has shaped as if he will be suited by greater tests of stamina. Henrietta Knight had a mixed season last term, but Somersby should be an exciting prospect for her in the current campaign and is very much one to follow. **Miss H C Knight**

Trainer comment: "The idea is for him to go novice chasing and start at two miles. He jumps as well, if not better, than Calgary Bay and has more speed than him too. The Arkle is the long-term objective."

Sona Sasta (Ire) h93p

6 b.g Sonus (Ire) – Derry Lark (Ire) (Lancastrian)
2008/9 19s 17s⁶ 17v⁴ Feb 5

David Pipe's stable experienced a mixed 2008/09 season, falling twenty-four short of its third consecutive century of winners since he took over the reins at Pond House Stables. But with a significant number of winners already on the board after a profitable summer jumps campaign, the stable's tally has the potential to bounce back, and one who should contribute to the total is the Sonus gelding Sona Sasta. Now qualified for handicaps, Sona Sasta is likely to reveal much more ability this winter than he had shown in three quick runs over hurdles at Taunton early in the year. The winner of an Irish point in May 2008, Sona Sasta showed his first form on his final outing, when fourth behind Carrickboy over a wholly inadequate trip. Significant improvement can be expected when Sona Sasta tackles distances of two and a half miles and more, and he'll be of particular interest once sent chasing. **D E Pipe**

Trainer comment: "He's not back in the yard yet. He could go over hurdles or fences, though he's bred to be a chaser. There may be better to come from him."

Tara Taylor   h96p F94
6 b.m Kayf Tara – Marielou (Fr) (Carwhite)
2008/9 F17s³ F16s F17s* 20d⁴ 19v³ 19d⁵ Mar 25

Any plans for a career in the paddocks can be put on the back-burner where Tara Taylor is concerned. A half-sister to two winning jumpers, including Dakota Girl who went on to produce the useful chaser Black Hills, Tara Taylor does have a future at stud. But, given the opportunities now available for mares over jumps, it's no surprise that she will continue racing for at least another season. Stamina very much won the day when Tara Taylor defied odds of 25/1 in a mares maiden bumper at Folkestone, and this daughter of Kayf Tara went on to shape like a stayer on all three starts over hurdles. A BHA mark of 97 certainly doesn't look beyond her judging by her final outing, when she was a fast-finishing fifth (beaten just two and a half lengths) in a conditional jockeys handicap at Towcester, where mistakes at the final two flights arguably proved costly. Tara Taylor seems sure to build on that form in 2009/10, particularly if upped to three miles. **C E Longsdon**

Trainer comment: "She should have won at Towcester on her last start when she was still last at the bottom of the hill. She'll need at least two and a half miles and I think she's got a stone in hand."

Tasheba   h139+
4 ch.g Dubai Destination (USA) – Tatanka (Ire) (Lear Fan (USA))
2008/9 16g² 19g* 17d* 19g³ Apr 25 :: 2009/10 NR (Jun20F⁴)

'How you start is important, but it is how you finish that counts—in the race for success, speed is less important than stamina.' So said the founder of capitalist magazine Forbes, business advice which has not been heeded by many of that publication's readership judging by the current global economic crisis. One way of bucking the credit crunch this winter, however, could be to follow the Nicky Henderson-trained Tasheba, a four-year-old gelding whose main asset is definitely stamina. That much was obvious from an early stage of his Flat career, which saw him win three times at up to fifteen furlongs for Peter Chapple-Hyam, showing a useful level of form in the process. Tasheba then made an excellent start over hurdles for his new stable in 2008/9, finishing runner-up in a highly-

Further wins should be on the cards for Tasheba this winter

competitive juvenile at Newbury prior to winning in good style at Ascot (maiden) and Cheltenham, looking a smart staying prospect on both occasions. He went on to show further improvement in a well-contested handicap at Sandown on the final day of 2008/9, when one of four different leaders on the run-in before having to settle for a close third behind Sangfroid. Tasheba remains with potential to progress further over hurdles once his stamina is tested more fully, particularly as he ran well when fourth to stable-companion Caracciola in the marathon Queen Alexandra Stakes at Royal Ascot on his return to the Flat in June.

N J Henderson

Trainer comment: "How far will he stay? That's the question, as I'm always reluctant to go three miles with a four-year-old. He did nothing wrong last season and he's done well physically."

The Jigsaw Man (Ire)　　　　　　　　　　　　　　　　　F114
5 ch.g Bob Back (USA) – Native Sunset (Ire) (Be My Native (USA))
2008/9 NR :: 2009/10 F16m* F16d² F16m* Sep 5

Rebecca Curtis features as one of the 'Future Stars' in this year's edition and the Pembrokeshire-based handler looks to have just the horse to take her training career to the next level in the shape of The Jigsaw Man. The Jigsaw Man, who made his debut only at the end of June, created a big impression in three starts in bumpers, winning twice at Stratford. He couldn't have been more impressive when beating Benbens ten lengths on the second occasion, going with stacks of enthusiasm in the lead and coasting clear from the home turn. In between, The Jigsaw Man was taken to Galway where he found only the very promising Loosen My Load, a gelding who features in this book's Irish subsection, too strong. The Jigsaw Man looks a most exciting hurdling prospect as, given his bumper record, he'll surely need to jump with only a reasonable degree of fluency to win decent novices. Although a full brother to Tisseman, a winning hurdler who stayed three miles, and out of a half-sister to the dual Cathcart winner Stormyfairweather, The Jigsaw Man hasn't looked short of speed by any means in bumpers. **Miss Rebecca Curtis**

Trainer comment: "He'll go novice hurdling now and is a brilliant jumper. He's very straightforward and seems to go on any ground. I think he's a two-miler."

Topjeu (Ire)　　　　　　　　　　　　　　　　　h110p
6 b.g Montjeu (Ire) – Arabian Lass (SAF) (Al Mufti (USA))
2008/9 17g⁴ 16g 16m 16s² Nov 18

The brilliant Montjeu, winner of eleven of his sixteen races, including the Prix de l'Arc de Triomphe and King George, has already sired two Derby winners, Motivator and Authorized, among a number of top performers on the Flat to date; and in Hurricane Fly he now has a potentially top-class hurdler. Topjeu doesn't feature in the top echelon of his sire's offspring under either code, but he was useful on the Flat and has the potential to reach a similar standard over hurdles, looking a sure-fire winner of handicaps in 2009/10. Few trainers are as good as Jonjo O'Neill when it comes to placing his handicappers, and there was clearly a good degree of confidence behind Topjeu when, following a trio of eye-catching runs in maiden/novice hurdle company, he made his handicap debut at Fakenham. He duly improved plenty to chase home Circus Rose there, and while those who took the 2/1 were left counting the cost, time clearly showed that Topjeu had plenty on at the weights that day conceding 8 lb to the winner, who followed up in a novice at Huntingdon. That performance also points to Topjeu being some way ahead of his new mark of 110; while there is still untapped potential trip-wise. Topjeu, who stays thirteen furlongs well on the Flat, has raced only around two miles over hurdles so far. **Jonjo O'Neill**

Trainer comment: "We'll keep him low key and he can win handicaps. He may stay further, too."

Touch of Irish   h120p
7 b.g Kayf Tara – Portland Row (Ire) (Zaffaran (USA))
2008/9 16g* 20m² Apr 20

Bumpers have long been a happy hunting ground for North Yorkshire trainer Alan Swinbank, with over 50% of his stable's wins during the last five National Hunt seasons having come in this sphere. Indeed, although Swinbank enjoys the bulk of his success on the Flat nowadays, stable stars such as Turbo Linn (2007 Lancashire Oaks winner) and Collier Hill (prolific globe-trotting Group winner) both began their careers in bumpers. This illustrious duo are prime examples of Swinbank's approach to bumpers, which he regularly targets with the late-maturing Flat-bred types (often bargain buys). 'They stand around for five minutes at the start in these bumpers and a lot of the runners are bred to win three-mile chases, so the mile-and-a-half horses can get away with the (two-mile) trip and it makes sense to pick up a bit of prize money while you're educating them.' Touch of Irish also hails from a Flat-oriented family, but he is still more stoutly bred (dam was a winning pointer) than most of his stable-companions, so hurdles were always likely to be on the agenda for this useful-looking gelding after a fine bumper campaign in 2007/8—he won twice at Newcastle prior to running well in graded events at Aintree (runner-up) and Punchestown (fifth). That Aintree race worked out well, with Cape Tribulation (third) and Copper Bleu (fifth) both developing into smart novice hurdlers last season. By contrast, Touch of Irish missed most of 2008/9, but he created a good impression when finally reappearing in a two-mile novice hurdle at Kelso in late-March, running out a wide-margin winner after being left clear two out when already on top. On the face of it, an odds-on defeat in similar company at Hexham on his only subsequent start was disappointing, yet Touch of Irish again impressed with the way he travelled through that race, whilst the combination of firmer ground and a second quick run after his lay-off probably told against him in the end. The BHA handicapper hasn't taken any chances with a mark of 130, but Touch of Irish's bumper form suggests he'll still prove competitive off that and he looks one to follow in handicap hurdles on the Northern circuit. **G A Swinbank**

Trainer comment: "He's coming on grand. He wants decent ground and should win his share."

Vamizi (Ire)   h108p
6 b.g Supreme Leader – Cuilin Bui (Ire) (Kemal (Fr))
2008/9 19s⁵ 20d⁴ Nov 26

The paradise island of Vamizi, off the coast of Mozambique, is about as far removed from a wild and woolly Wednesday in January at Newbury as it is possible to get. However, it was on such a day at the Berkshire track that Vamizi's half-brother King Harald first announced himself as a well above-average chaser in 2004/5, and it will more than likely be under similar conditions that Vamizi makes his mark over fences this season. Having finished third on his sole outing in a bumper, Vamizi shaped with plenty of promise on both starts in novice hurdles last November, notably when fourth to Bensalem at Chepstow. After reportedly suffering a slight setback subsequently, he's now likely to be fast-tracked to novice chases, something he has all the attributes to suggest will suit, with a step up to three miles also looking made to measure. **M Bradstock**

Trainer comment: "He went a bit lame behind which is why he didn't run after November last season, but he's absolutely fine now. He'll go straight over fences."

Vino Griego (Fr)   F112
4 b.g Kahyasi – Vie de Reine (Fr) (Mansonnien (Fr))
2008/9 F12s² F16s* Feb 14

It took a bid of €65,000 to secure Vino Griego when he came up for sale as a two-year-old in France in 2007, though in the light of his performances to date connections won't be regretting a cent of it. He showed himself a smart prospect in two starts in bumpers, and has plenty going for him as he embarks on his career over jumps. Well supported on his debut over a mile and a half at Newbury in January, Vino Griego battled on well to finish a length behind Zazamix. A month later he impressed when going one better over two miles at Ascot, in a race where three of his rivals had winning form beforehand. Vino Griego travelled strongly under a hold-up ride and quickly opened a clear gap when asked to quicken, running on well despite edging right. His nearest pursuer Western Leader, who was six lengths adrift, gave the form a boost when winning at Limerick in March. Vino Griego is the first foal of Vie de Reine, a fairly useful hurdler/chaser around two and a half miles in France. Likely to stay further than two miles himself, Vino Griego looks an exciting prospect for novice hurdles this season. **G L Moore**

Trainer comment: "I'm very much looking forward to him—he's done well over the summer. He'll start at two miles, but I do think he'll stay further."

Wymott (Ire) F100

5 b.g Witness Box (USA) – Tanya Thyne (Ire) (Good Thyne (USA))
2008/9 F16s^2 F17g* F17d Apr 4

Trevor Hemmings has invested substantial amounts of money into building his string of racehorses into one of the major powers of National Hunt racing, and the Lancashire-born business tycoon has been rewarded with numerous high-profile successes, the most notable being the 2005 Grand National victory of Hedgehunter. Hemmings has his horses spread amongst various trainers across Britain and Ireland, one of them being Donald McCain Jnr whose winners for Hemmings in 2008/9 included the promising five-year-old Wymott. The fact that Wymott was sent off favourite for his debut in a bumper at Catterick in January suggested he was well regarded by connections and, despite clear signs of greenness, he produced a good performance to finish runner-up to subsequent dual-winner Saveiro. McCain's charge then recorded his maiden success seven weeks later when powering away in good style at Bangor, despite having looked as though he would prove ideally suited by a much truer test. Last season ended with a respectable mid-field finish in the Aintree bumper, and significant improvement can be expected once Wymott is stepped up in trip and faced with hurdles this campaign. **D McCain Jnr**

Trainer comment: (See trainer interview, p71)

SPECIAL OFFER
UP TO £20 FREE FOR EVERY READER AT TIMEFORM.COM

Simply buy up to £20 of credit at timeform.com before the end of 2009 and we will add the same amount again to the balance of your account.

Your free £20 could be used to download 4 Timeform Race Cards or why not try our new Race Passes for a couple of days?

Remember you can also download each issue of Horses To Follow Extra for only £5.

Just enter the code HTFJ20 when you make your deposit. If you don't have a timeform.com account already registration is straight-forward and free! Follow the instructions at timeform.com.

*Free credit must be used within 6 months. Offer applies online at timeform.com and no alternative is available. Promotional code may be used once per customer. See timeform.com/terms.asp for full conditions and terms of use.

THE HOME OF WINNERS SINCE 1948

Horses To Follow From Ireland

Askthemaster (Ire)   c125
9 b.g Oscar (Ire) – Nicola Mac (Ire) (King's Ride)
2008/9 c17v^5 c19d^F c20v^6 c24v :: 2009/10 c17s* May 4

There are often two views that can be taken when it comes to a horse being lightly raced. The negative one might be to suggest it has had training problems and, therefore, can't stand repeated racing, but those for whom the glass is usually half full can point to a lack of racing meaning untapped potential. The relatively-unexposed Askthemaster will hopefully conform to the latter school of thought, as merely giving his running from his current chase mark is likely to see him winning a handicap or two, so well treated does he appear starting out in 2009/10. The nine-year-old has had only three more starts than his age to date, which emphasises how little racing he's had, yet he's rarely failed to fire when making it to the track and his reappearance win in a Limerick maiden chase in May emphasised the point; he made smooth headway from mid-field and didn't need to leave the bridle to resist Tryptronic, who went one better at Ballinrobe on his next outing. Askthemaster certainly looked to fit the 'improving' bill that day, and he could develop into a useful novice this season. His stamina is proven at up to two and a half miles, and he has raced only on ground softer than good.
Robert Tyner

Drunken Sailor (Ire)   h124p
4 b.g Tendulkar (USA) – Ronni Pancake (Mujadil (USA))
2008/9 16s* 16s^2 16d^6 Dec 26 :: 2009/10 NR ((Sep19F^2)

In short, put it in the 2009/10 Timeform Horses to Follow. That's our simple answer, anyway, to the question posed in the famous old sea shanty 'What Shall We Do With A Drunken Sailor?' Unlike the seafarers the piece refers to, though, it's the skills of trainer Paul Flynn rather than alcohol that are likely to spur this Drunken Sailor on to success and ensure he makes his presence felt in handicaps in 2009/10. Drunken Sailor created a good impression in his first season over timber, winning a juvenile at Gowran on his hurdling debut before splitting Tharawaat and fellow Irish 'Horse To Follow' Tilabay in a graded similar event at Fairyhouse in late-November. He failed to improve further when sixth at Leopardstown on his final outing, but there's reason to forgive that run bearing in mind how freely he raced early on, while his Flat form also provides plenty of hope he'll soon resume his progress. During his first spell hurdling, Drunken Sailor's Timeform Flat rating was a mere 86 and he was unproven beyond a mile, but he's added a stone to that figure already in 2009 and the step up to a mile and a half plus has doubtless played more than a small part in that. As such, his hurdles mark looks even more lenient now and there's obviously scope for him with a view to longer trips, having done his racing over hurdles around two miles. Drunken Sailor is versatile as regards ground, too, having shown his form in both spheres on soft and on the Flat on good to firm, and he's tough and genuine for all he wears headgear. ***Paul Flynn***

Jaffonnien (Fr) h119p
6 b.g Mansonnien (Fr) – Ostenne (Fr) (Rose Laurel)
2008/9 16v^6 16s^5 16s^F Feb 22

As National Hunt pedigrees go, not many are as speedy as Jaffonnien's. By Mansonnien, who numbers smart types such as Taranis and J'Y Vole amongst his progeny, Jaffonnien hails from a family of out-and-out two milers on the dam's side of his pedigree, including Ostenne herself, as well as half-brothers Stenborg and Stenbreeze. Jaffonnien's future almost certainly lies around the minimum trip, too, and it's a future that looks bright with an eye on 2009/10. There'll be bigger targets later on should everything go smoothly, but the starting point for this term will no doubt be to win a hurdle race, which should be little more than a formality based on the form (and promise) he showed in three runs over timber in 2008/9 on the back of his useful debut success in a bumper at Leopardstown the previous season. Jaffonnien kept good company for each of his hurdle runs and didn't once look out of place; he caught the eye behind useful types Academy Sir Harry and Fisher Bridge on his hurdling debut, made most when fifth in a listed novice at Punchestown (Go Native first, China Rock second) next time, and was going as well as any when falling two out in a maiden won in a good time by Smoking Aces at Naas on his most recent appearance. Jaffonnien is fairly useful already, and his bumper form, allied with such a promising start over hurdles, suggests he's going to prove even better this time around, with chasing a valid option as well should connections choose. ***A L T Moore***

Jessies Dream (Ire)   141p F106
6 ch.g Presenting – Lady Apprentice (Ire) (Phardante (Fr))
2008/9 F19v* 18s* :: 2009/10 20s* Apr 30

That Jessies Dream had a fair amount of ability was obvious when he started out as a five-year-old, winning a point and finishing in the frame in a couple of bumpers in three runs for Paul Cashman, yet there was nothing to suggest that about a year later, having joined Willie Mullins in the meantime, he would be regarded as one of the most promising jumpers in Ireland.

Jessies Dream is unbeaten in three runs for Mullins, showing much improved form to get off the mark in a bumper at Naas in January then successful over hurdles in a maiden at Thurles in February and a minor event at Punchestown in April. A horse who has tended to race freely and who made the running at Thurles, Jessies Dream, with Ruby Walsh on board for the first time, settled well at Punchestown. The good gallop there certainly helped in that respect, and Walsh was able to ride a patient race. Still with plenty to do three out, Jessies Dream made rapid headway to chase the leaders after the next and burst through a gap to settle the issue in a matter of strides before the last, very untidy there but still winning impressively by four lengths from Noble Prince. A lengthy, good-topped invididual from the family of the Queen Mother Champion Chase winner Buck House, Jessies Dream is now set to go over fences and he looks a most exciting chasing prospect, one who will stay three miles. He has done all of his racing so far on soft or heavy ground. **W P Mullins**

Lenabane (Ire)   h133
7 b.g Luso – Meelick Lady (Ire) (Duky)
2008/9 $16s^2$ $16s^4$ $16s^4$ $16d^4$ $16s^6$ $20s^2$ 20d* $20g^3$ Apr 14

Seven wins from twelve starts over hurdles and unbeaten the first nineteen times he completed over fences, including two Champion Chases and a Tingle Creek rightly dubbed one of the great races of the modern era. That's not a work of fiction, just the phenomenal race record of Moscow Flyer, Jessica Harrington's outstanding chaser, whose half-brother Lenabane is fully expected to make into a leading novice chaser in 2009/10. The trainer is different, Dessie Hughes rather than Harrington, and the level of ability concerned is likely to be a little way removed as well, but Lenabane has achieved almost as much as Moscow Flyer did in his first season over hurdles. Like his illustrious relative, he's effective at two miles to two and a half miles and, as a tall, lengthy individual, he has always looked the type to be seen to even better advantage over fences. As might be expected of a seven-year-old in only his second season on the track, Lenabane was getting the hang of hurdling only as 2008/9 was drawing to a close, opening his account at the eighth time of asking when beating the useful Uimhiraceathair in a maiden at Gowran, and leaving even that form behind to chase home Oscar Dan Dan and Caim Hill in a Fairyhouse Grade 2 on his final appearance. Lenabane should hit the ground running this time around, as happened with Moscow Flyer in his second full campaign. ***D T Hughes***

Loosen My Load (Ire) h117P F115
5 b.g Dushyantor (USA) – The Kids Dante (Ire) (Phardante (Fr))
2009/10 F16m* F16d* 16d* Sep 16

Sizing Europe provided trainer Henry de Bromhead with his biggest success to date when winning the Irish Champion Hurdle in 2007/8 and, while that one looks an exciting chasing prospect this season, his owners can look forward to picking up some more prizes over the smaller obstacles with Loosen My Load, who made a successful hurdling debut in a maiden at Listowel.

Prior to that victory, Loosen My Load had created a very good impression in winning both his bumper starts, justifying favouritism easily at Cork on his debut and improving on that form when beating no less than five last-time-out winners (and two subsequent ones) in what is traditionally a strong event at the Galway Festival in August. A big gelding, it bodes well that Loosen My Load's two bumper wins came on sharp tracks; neither run would have got to the bottom of him, and it says plenty for his ability that he was able to overhaul British-raider, and member of the 'Fifty', The Jigsaw Man at Galway, despite losing ground and momentum when running wide on the home turn. Conversely, Loosen My Load's first attempt over hurdles could hardly have gone more smoothly. He impressed greatly with his jumping and needed little more than shaking up to draw clear of fairly useful Flat performer Luzdeluna and sixteen others.

Bought for €82,000 as a 3-y-o, Loosen My Load is out of an unraced sister to fairly useful chaser Young Dubliner and hails from an excellent jumping family that includes very smart chaser Everett and smart hurdler/high-class chaser Cab On Target. He can be expected to stay at least two and a half miles and looks one of the most exciting prospects around for novice hurdling. ***Henry de Bromhead***

Luska Lad (Ire)   F120
5 ch.g Flemensfirth (USA) – Notsophar (Ire) (Phardante (Fr))
2008/9 F17g F16v* F16s* F16s* F16v^2 F16m* :: 2009/10 F16s^2 Apr 29

Few horses will have run in as many bumpers as Luska Lad, who was having his eighth start in that sphere when chasing home subsequently-disqualified Dunguib and fellow member of the 'Fifteen' Sweeps Hill in the Championship event at Punchestown very early this season. The extra experience he's gained is sure to stand him in good stead for his upcoming hurdling campaign, and he's just the type to win good races in novice company. Luska Lad's early efforts were pretty low-key, but he positively flourished last autumn, completing a hat-trick when making all at Fairyhouse in November. Thereafter, only the aforementioned duo got the better of him, with Dunguib also taking his measure at Navan before Christmas. If anything, Luska Lad's form was improving by the time his stint in bumpers came to an end. Luska Lad's pedigree has prospective jumper written all over it as well. His dam, who was of little account herself, is a half-sister to smart chaser Fota Island and closely related to good-class staying hurdlers Castlekelly Leader and Black Jack Ketchum, while his sire Flemensfirth has developed into one of the leading National Hunt stallions of the time. The good-topped Luska Lad has the size to take to hurdling, too, and he's sure to stay two and a half miles.
John Joseph Hanlon

Mask of Darkness (Ire)   h120p c92p
6 b.g Moscow Society (USA) – Barnearrig Lass (Ire) (Pollerton)
2008/9 20v 17s 20s 20v^5 16s 24v^3 20d* c17d :: 2009/10 c19s c17s May 24

Mask of Darkness is probably well named, given there's more than a feeling we haven't yet seen anything like his true colours, over hurdles or fences; in Timeform's view, he's going to be useful when he finally does reveal his all. His record is pretty chequered on the face of it, but suffice to say Mask of Darkness has looked good the times he has been on his game, starting when he justified favouritism in a Gowran Park bumper in March 2008. Mask of Darkness' early hurdles efforts were eye-catching, and the move for him in the betting prior to a maiden at Chepstow in January was even more so. The gamble went astray as it happened, but only because Mask of Darkness found his stamina stretched upped to three miles on testing ground and, having travelled best that day, he duly made amends returned to shorter at Leopardstown six weeks later when beating three next-time-out winners with something to spare. There's little doubt we've still to see the best of Mask of Darkness over hurdles, but three quick, down-the-field runs in maiden chases should ensure he's allotted a chase mark that wholly underplays his ability and, given his shrewd stable, any market move for him in handicaps will be well worth following. **Charles Byrnes**

Oscar Rebel (Ire) h140 c126p

7 b.m Oscar (Ire) – Be My Baltic (Ire) (Be My Native (USA))
2008/9 18d c20v³ 21v² 20d 22g :: 2009/10 18s⁵ c20ᶠ May 15

A losing run of seven is hardly the record one would ordinarily look for in a horse gaining its second successive inclusion in this section, but we feel Oscar Rebel is well worth another chance to pay her way in 2009/10. This good-topped mare was picked for last year's book on the back of a fine novice hurdle campaign in 2007/8, when her three wins included valuable Grade 3 mares events at Fairyhouse and Punchestown, and she appealed as one who would do at least as well over fences. Unfortunately, Oscar Rebel's chasing campaign proved to be a short-lived affair, as connections opted to send her back over hurdles (without success despite showing useful form) after finishing a promising third in a listed mares maiden at Clonmel in November. Indeed, Oscar Rebel wasn't seen over

Useful mare Oscar Rebel (stars on cap) looks well worth persevering with over fences

fences again until mid-May, when she fell at the fourth last in a mares novice at Cork, looking the most likely winner at the time. Of course, there's a chance that spill will have dented Oscar Rebel's confidence, but her jumping has been pretty assured otherwise (she was a winning pointer prior to being sent under Rules) and the chances are she'll be gaining compensation sooner rather than later.
W J Burke

Pandorama (Ire)   h152 F116

6 b.g Flemensfirth (USA) – Gretchen's Castle (Ire) (Carlingford Castle)
2008/9 F19s* 20v* 20v* 20v² 18s* Feb 15

In terms of winners, last season wasn't a particularly memorable one for Noel Meade, his final tally of sixty-two his second lowest total since 1996/7 and falling some way short of the total achieved by Willie Mullins. As the saying goes, though, every cloud has a silver lining, and there were some notable highs along the way, notably Go Native's victory in the Supreme Novices' Hurdle at Cheltenham, the triumphant return of the much-heralded Aran Concerto and the emergence of a potential star in the making in the shape of Pandorama.

The winner of a point and two bumpers, Pandorama wasted no time in establishing himself as one of the leading staying novice hurdlers in Ireland

Pandorama (noseband) takes full advantage of Cousin Vinny's unlucky departure

during 2008/9 and he produced possibly the most visually impressive performance of the campaign on that side of the Irish Sea when demolishing Alpha Ridge, himself seeking a four-timer, on just his second start over timber in the 'Monksfield' Novices' Hurdle at Navan. Pandorama was found to be lame after failing in his attempt to give the then little-known Mikael d'Haguenet 4 lb on the same course next time, but he got back on track when winning the Grade 1 Deloitte Novices' Hurdle at Leopardstown on his final start of the season. Admittedly, he was a shade fortunate—Cousin Vinny had just loomed alongside and was about to take his measure when crashing out at the final flight—but two and a quarter miles on such a flat track was never likely to play to Pandorama's strengths and there was more than enough in his performance to suggest he's set to continue his rise in 2009/10.

A relentless galloper from the family of the smart staying hurdler Mrs Muck, Pandorama has all the attributes to go right to the top in novice chases this term, with three miles on testing ground (the latter is rarely in short supply in Ireland) likely to prove his optimum conditions. **N Meade**

Pesoto (Fr) h118 c123p
6 gr.g Lesotho (USA) – Istoire (Fr) (Dadarissime (Fr))
2008/9 19s^F c20s^2 c17d^6 16g Apr 13

With form figures for last season reading 'F260', the Edward O'Grady-trained Pesoto might not be an obvious choice as one to follow, but he did more than enough in those four starts to suggest he remains one to keep on side in 2009/10.

Successful three times on the Flat, and on his sole start over hurdles for previous connections in France, Pesoto shaped promisingly a couple of times last term, notably when a close second to the now smart chaser Joncol at Punchestown on his chasing debut. A free-going front runner who's likely to prove best around 2m with the emphasis is on speed, Pesoto was simply outstayed by the winner on that occasion having arguably gone off too hard in front, though it reflects well that he still managed to pull well clear of the remainder. Pesoto had valid excuses on both subsequent starts, too, out of his depth in the Grade 1 Durkan New Homes Novices' Chase at Leopardstown and seeming amiss when sent back over hurdles on his final outing almost four months later.

Edward O'Grady has traditionally done well with his French imports in the past, the 2006 Coral Cup winner Sky's The Limit the most high-profile in recent years, and the fluent-jumping Pesoto looks sure to pick up a 2m maiden or novice chase before going on to better things in handicaps. **E J O'Grady**

Sports Line (Ire)   h143p
6 b.g Norwich – Hot Line (Ire) (Riverhead (USA))
2008/9 16d² 16s* 16s* Mar 14

Willie Mullins has clearly been one of the leading trainers in Ireland for many years now, but in recent times, as the quality of horse in his Closutton yard has improved, he has really propelled himself to the next level. Success breeds success, as the old adage goes, and there are plenty of reasons to believe 2009/10 is going to be at least as good for the reigning Irish Champion Trainer.

An amazing thirty-eight of last season's career-best tally of one hundred and twenty-five winners in Ireland came in bumpers, whilst his novice hurdlers swept all before them as well, so it was no surprise the likes of Mikael d'Haguenet, Hurricane Fly and Cousin Vinny grabbed the majority of the headlines, but there were many more potential stars bubbling just under the surface, and one that really caught the eye was Sports Line.

A lightly-raced son of Norwich, Sports Line has made rapid strides over hurdles so far. He started 2008/9 with a rather unlucky short-head defeat at Cork, and wasted no time putting that right when making all to beat subsequent dual winner Dundrum easily by three and a half lengths at Punchestown. Sports Line jumped markedly left that day, so it was no surprise his next start came at left-handed Naas, and he could hardly have been more impressive, barely needing to come off the bridle to trounce the previous season's Champion Bumper runner-up Corskeagh Royale by fifteen lengths. His build (tall, good-topped) and style of racing mark him down as a cracking prospect for fences this term, and his dam is a half-sister to the useful chaser up to 3m Terao. Sports Line has yet to try further than two and a half miles himself, but he'll stay longer distances if learning to settle. ***W P Mullins***

Sweeps Hill (NZ)   F116
5 b.g Montjeu (Ire) – Windfield Dancer (NZ) (Zabeel (NZ))
2008/9 F16d* :: 2009/10 F16s* Apr 29

New Zealand is, unsurprisingly, still associated far more with Rugby and Cricket on the sporting front, but it's very easy to forget just how much success horses bred in that country have had in Britain and Ireland since the globetrotting Grand Canyon set the ball rolling in the late-'seventies. Royal Mail (Whitbread), Playschool (Hennessy) and Seagram (Grand National) are three notable New Zealand-breds who have won big races over jumps in the past thirty years, and it's not beyond the bounds of possibility that Sweeps Hill could match their achievements one day. He already has one major prize under his belt, having been awarded the Champion Bumper at Punchestown in May following the disqualification of Dunguib, who failed a dope test.

It was during a purple period for trainer John Kiely when Sweeps Hill made a successful start to his career in a bumper at Leopardstown in late-2008/9, but he showed he was full value and more for that comfortable defeat of previous winners when next seen at the latest Punchestown Festival, getting closest (beaten nine lengths) to the Cheltenham Champion Bumper winner Dunguib. The tall, good-topped Sweeps Hill really took the eye beforehand at Punchestown, looking every inch a jumper in the making, and he's the type to win good novice hurdles this year; don't be surprised to see him featuring again at the top festivals come the spring, with trips beyond two miles unlikely to trouble him. **John E Kiely**

Taipan's Way (Ire)   c136p
7 b.g Taipan (Ire) – Wayward Bride (Ire) (Shernazar)
2008/9 c20s c21s^F c21s^4 c20v* c17g* Apr 13

A fast-improving chaser who was successful on his last two starts in his novice season, and now looks set to go on and win good-quality handicaps at up to two and a half miles. That's Taipans's Way, a seven-year-old who for long enough appeared to be one of the lesser lights in the Willie Mullins yard, with just one win in bumpers and one over hurdles followed by defeats on his first three appearances over fences.

Taipan's Way did catch the eye on the last of those aforementioned runs over fences, and next time showed that he was finally getting his act together when winning a maiden at Limerick in January. He was to make an even bigger step forward on his only subsequent appearance, in a thirteen-runner novice handicap at Fairyhouse in April, for which he started favourite. Jumping well throughout this time, Taipan's Way travelled strongly, as he usually does, and took up the running before five out, only really coming off the bridle after the last when top weight Rock Street threatened briefly, going on to score by four and a half lengths. A big gelding with plenty of scope for further improvement, Taipan's Way did virtually all of his racing in bumpers on good and good to firm ground. He has raced only on good or softer over jumps, winning on heavy at Limerick. **W P Mullins**

Tilabay (Ire) h129p

4 b.g Sadler's Wells (USA) – Tilimsana (Ire) (Darshaan)
2008/9 16s 16s³ 16d⁴ 16s⁵ :: 2009/10 16d* Sep 14

Such has been Willie Mullins' dominance on the Irish National Hunt scene that it's understandable why owners might want to seek out his services. Connections of Barker have certainly had little cause to regret their decision to change stables last winter, with the gelding developing into a leading novice chaser when winning three of his four starts (including the Grade 1 Swordlestown) after joining Mullins. A similar switch with Tilabay is already reaping rewards. Since leaving Adrian Sexton in the summer, Tilabay has shown improved form to win a mile-and-a-half maiden on the Flat at Wexford in August and a valuable four-year-old handicap hurdle over two miles at Listowel in September. Admittedly, the gelding faces a hike in the weights for that latter win, but he won it in sufficiently good style—beating Siberian Tiger comfortably by two lengths despite a mistake at the last—to suggest he'll continue to be of interest for a good while longer. Indeed, his style of victory was reminiscent of Mullins' 2008 winner of the same race, Sesenta, who has since developed into a useful performer, claiming very valuable handicap wins over both hurdles (Whitewater Shopping Centre Hurdle at Punchestown) and on the Flat (Ebor at York). It wouldn't be a surprise if the well-bred Tilabay, whose grandam was the high-class Flat performer Timarida, followed a similar route over the coming months. **W P Mullins**

MORE IRISH WINNERS ON THE CARDS

TIMEFORM RACE CARDS ARE AVAILABLE FOR EVERY MEETING EVERY DAY

£5 each at timeform.com

THE HOME OF WINNERS SINCE 1948

Interview
Philip Hobbs

A new addition to the Timeform Betfair Racing Club training ranks, Philip Hobbs has been towards the head of the National Hunt Trainers' Championship for well over a decade, reaching over a hundred winners in a remarkable nine of the last ten seasons. Hobbs's best campaign came in 2002/3, when Cheltenham Festival heroes Rooster Booster and One Knight helped the Minehead trainer amass one hundred and thirty-four winners, and Hobbs has been responsible for plenty of other recent big-race winners as well, amongst them Flagship Uberalles, Farmer Jack and Monkerhostin, all of whom were ridden to success at one time or another by stable jockey Richard Johnson, in many eyes the best rider never to have won a jockeys' title. In Johnson's absence, Tom O'Brien picks up the bulk of the yard's rides, though in stable conditional Rhys Flint they also boast arguably the most promising young rider around. Hobbs kindly took time out of his busy pre-season schedule (which includes the odd Flat runner) to run through some of his big hopes for 2009/10.

Fair Along (Ger) (h158 c148) 7 b.g Alkalde (Ger) – Fairy Tango (Fr) (Acatenango (Ger)) 2008/9 21g² 25s* 24s* 24v³ 24d 24g³ :: 2009/10 24s Apr 30. The plan is to run in the Cesarewitch (at Newmarket) first and then go to Wetherby for the three-mile conditions hurdle (West Yorkshire Hurdle) on the last Saturday of the month, which is a Grade 2. We're open minded after that. If he was still a

Promising conditional Rhys Flint has struck up a good relationship with stable stalwart Fair Along

novice, I'd very much look at the chase option, but he's not and he has a high handicap mark over fences in any case. How he runs in those first two races will make our minds up for the rest of the season—he's looking as enthusiastic as ever.

Snap Tie (Ire) (h151) 7 b.g Pistolet Bleu (Ire) – Aries Girl (Valiyar) 2008/9 16m* 16g² 16d³ 16d 16m⁶ Apr 18. He might be the best I suppose. Maybe, in retrospect, we did the wrong thing last season staying over hurdles, but he wasn't far off the top end. Now he'll definitely go novice chasing, and he's schooled very well already. He'll be running, I hope, by the end of October, but he does not want the ground too soft, that's the problem. I hope he could be an Arkle type, but we'll just start low and go from there.

A novice chase campaign is on the cards for the smart Snap Tie

Ring The Boss (Ire) (h150 c137) 8 b.g Kahyasi – Fortune's Girl (Ardross) 2008/9 c20g* c21s² c20d⁴ c20v* c21d Mar 12. I thought he was very disappointing last season because I thought at the start of the campaign he was our best novice chase prospect. Although he won two and performed fairly well, he wasn't top end. He lacks a bit of bottle I think, so we might go back to handicap hurdles with him. He's very effective at two miles on bottomless ground, but I think on better ground he needs two and a half.

Planet of Sound (c147) 7 b.g Kayf Tara – Herald The Dawn (Dubassoff (USA)) 2008/9 c16d⁴ c18d* c18s* c16d³ c20g³ Apr 2. He seems to be very well. I think the obvious route for him is the Haldon Gold Cup at Exeter, for a couple of reasons really; he's not going to be competitive in a conditions chase from the mark he's on at the moment, so it makes sense to start in a handicap and off a BHA mark of 152 he's bound to be in the weights. The other thing is we're not really sure what his trip is and Exeter's a stiff two and a quarter, so that may decide which way to go afterwards. He disappointed at Aintree when last out, but he's certainly in good form now.

Massini's Maguire (Ire) (c146) 8 b.g Dr Massini (Ire) – Molly Maguire (Ire) (Supreme Leader) 2008/9 c21g* c24g² c20d² c24d³ c25d⁵ Apr 3. He passed his scan just yesterday on a hind leg which was the problem after Aintree, so now he's back in more serious work, but he won't be running until December, probably Christmas. Off 149 he's some way off those conditions chases, so again we'll have to start in a handicap. Distance-wise I'm not too sure; I thought he got the trip well enough in the RSA before disappointing at Aintree, but I think we'll ideally start at two mile six furlongs.

Ballydub (Ire) (h145) 6 b.g Presenting – Sovereign Leader (Ire) (Supreme Leader) 2008/9 21s² 24s* 24dᶠ 22d² 24d Mar 12. He'll go three-mile novice chasing and he wants soft ground. I've got just a little bit of a niggle about his jumping as he's sometimes very careful over hurdles, but you would hope he'd be a very decent novice if he gets that side of it together. He's promising, and we're just hoping that chasing could be the making of him; he's a big strong horse, and should certainly jump fences.

Prince Taime (Fr) (h142) 6 b.g Astarabad (USA) – Maite (Fr) (Valdingran (Fr)) 2008/9 16s³ 16d 16g³ 20m* 20g² :: 2009/10 20g² May 2. I thought we'd probably start him in a hurdle race as he's rated 145 by the BHA handicapper, and if he were to go and win he'd be 155 and not far off those conditions hurdles. If he doesn't go and win convincingly first time then he'll be running over fences. He improved so much in the spring because he started settling better, in his home work as well. He's not short of speed and I wouldn't have thought he'd want more than two and a half miles.

Tarablaze (h136p) 6 b.g Kayf Tara – Princess Hotpot (Ire) (King's Ride) 2008/9 22d* 20d² 20s* 25s* Feb 14. He'll go straight novice chasing over three miles—he definitely stays well. He's won a point to point in Ireland already, and he's the opposite from Snap Tie because he goes very well on soft ground. He's very genuine.

Kornati Kid (c133p) 7 b.g Kayf Tara – Hiltonstown Lass (Ire) (Denel (Fr)) 2008/9 c24d² c24d⁴ c24s* c25s* c32d⁶ Mar 11. He definitely wants a long distance and I would have thought the Welsh National could well be a possibility with him, as he also wants soft ground. He's genuine and tries very hard, and had probably had enough for the season when he ran at Cheltenham on his final start.

Lead On (Ire) (h125) 8 b.g Supreme Leader – Dressed In Style (Ire) (Meneval (USA)) 2008/9 20d⁶ 19d Jan 17. Well I'm just hoping we've got things back on track. He won a decent novice chase at Cheltenham and then we had problems afterwards—he was never moving properly, and since then he's had an operation on a knee. We're hoping that's put things right again, as he's cantering well now. He'd be a horse for the better handicap chases, but we'll probably start back in a hurdle race. He may be ready for the Silver Trophy at Chepstow again (runner-up in 2007).

Spanish Conquest (h119) 5 b.g Hernando (Fr) – Sirena (Ger) (Tejano (USA)) 2008/9 17s⁶ 17s 16s 16g* 16m* 17f* 19g Apr 25. He's very interesting because he's had a breathing operation since last season. He won those three races in ten days (in 2008/9) and travelled amazingly well in that two-and-a-half-mile handicap at Sandown until his breathing gave out and he couldn't get home, so he could still be well handicapped. We're very likely to try that trip again.

Timeform Betfair Racing Club

Unnamed 4 b.g Saddlers' Hall – Silver Glen (Roselier) He's a brother to Pause And Clause of Emma Lavelle's. He's cantering and doing a fair bit already, so I would hope he's a horse we hopefully don't have to wait too long for; he should be running in bumpers in November. It's very likely jumping will prove the making of him, and bloodstock agent Aidan Murphy, who bought the horse, thinks a fair bit of him and we're hoping he can be as nice as his brother.

Interview
Alan King

Paul Nicholls has undoubtedly been the dominant force in National Hunt racing since the turn of the century, accumulating more than 1200 winners and four Trainers' Championships during that period, but if anybody is going to halt the Nicholls bandwagon then Alan King is clearly the most likely candidate. King has been established towards the upper echelon of the sport for some time, yet his stock continues on the rise as his partnership with stable jockey Robert 'Choc ' Thornton flourishes, reaching triple-figures for winners in the last two seasons and eclipsing his 2007/8 total during the latest campaign with one hundred and thirty-six, just nineteen shy of Nicholls. Big-race success has been frequent in recent seasons, with Cheltenham Festival winners Voy Por Ustedes, Katchit and My Way de Solzen the yard's figureheads, and there are plenty of promising youngsters in King's care all set to make their presence felt at the top level in times ahead as well. King, therefore, was a natural choice for one of the Timeform Betfair Racing Club's newest additions, and he spoke to us recently to assess his burgeoning string.

Voy Por Ustedes (Fr) (c170) 8 b.g Villez (USA) – Nuit d'Ecajeul (Fr) (Matahawk) 2008/9 c20s⁴ c24g³ c21s* c21d² c20d* Apr 3. The first part of the season is the most difficult. After Christmas it's pretty much the same as last year, in that we'll go Ascot, Ryanair (at Cheltenham), Aintree—we just haven't really made our mind up as to where we'll start him. I'm slightly concerned if we go back to the Old Roan (at Aintree) that he's going to have a hard race giving weight away. The Peterborough at Huntingdon is an interesting race in December—two and a half miles would suit him ideally—but we'd just have to decide with Sir Robert (Ogden) if we wanted to tackle the King George; if we did, the Peterborough is probably too close. Apart from that he's in great form; it seems strange to say for a

The Betfair Ascot Chase is again likely to be a target for stable star Voy Por Ustedes

horse of his age, but he looks stronger than he's ever done, very powerful. We gave him only the five runs last season and I'm hopeful there's still plenty left in the tank.

Halcon Genelardais (Fr) (c165) 9 ch.g Halcon – Francetphile (Fr) (Farabi) 2008/9 c27s² c29d³ c25v² c26d^{pu} Mar 13. We're targeting the Welsh National again. He's a horse that loves to be fresh and he'll have only one run beforehand, which may even be in a handicap hurdle, possibly that Betfair fixed-brush race at Haydock he won three years ago. I'd really love to go to Chepstow all guns blazing and he'll still run extremely well despite his mark. One place I will avoid with him is Cheltenham. For whatever reason he never travels around there and ends up having a very hard race—even over three and a half miles at the Open meeting there last November he was off the bridle from the word go. After the Welsh National there's a chance, if the right race comes up, we may go to Ireland with him; the deep ground would suit him very well and some of those races cut up to very small fields.

Katchit (Ire) (h158) 6 b.g Kalanisi (Ire) – Miracle (Ezzoud (Ire)) 2008/9 16m² 16s³ 16d⁴ 16d⁶ 20d Apr 4. He's back in tremendous form. We've given him a long break and he's really in top order at the minute. We're going to step up to two and a half miles, certainly starting at that trip, with a view that we might even end up over three miles. I think he's just lost a bit of his dash, I certainly don't think it's lack

Longer trips are on the agenda now for Katchit, still without a win since this 2008 Champion Hurdle success

of effort on his part; in the Champion Hurdle he was flat out from halfway and did very well to finish sixth. I tried him in headgear at home and it didn't make one bit of difference, so I think it's just a case he's going as fast as he can and isn't quite quick enough now. There's a race at Ascot in November and we'll possibly go from there.

Karabak (Fr) (h151p F105) 6 b.g Kahyasi – Mosstraye (Fr) (Tip Moss (Fr)) 2008/9 F17g^3 19g^2 17s* 19d* 21d^2 24d^4 Apr 3. He was always a bit on the light side last year and he's done particularly well this summer. Like Katchit, we'll probably start at two and half miles with a view to stepping him up again, and I'd like to think he may develop into a World Hurdle horse. He's got to improve the best part of a stone to be up there, but he could easily do it and I don't think we've seen the best of him. He's possibly a bit stronger this time, but I still think he wants a month, six weeks between runs—Aintree probably came plenty quick enough for him last season after Cheltenham. I'm delighted with the way he looks and I think we could be in for a decent season with him.

Blazing Bailey (h149+) 7 b.g Mister Baileys – Wannaplantatree (Nininski (USA)) 2008/9 24s^4 25d^4 24v^6 24d 24s^4 Apr 17. He's interesting. He's not back yet and he disappointed me hugely last season, despite the fact his homework was the best it had ever been. We subsequently found he's possibly had a wind problem, and he's due to have his soft palate cauterized in the middle of October. It just might be the answer and, though he made no noise in his races, it has been proven in the last few years that they don't have to make a noise to be displacing. There's just a chance that it's been stopping him. The plan eventually is to go over fences, but if we're happy with him his comeback will be in the Long Distance Hurdle at Newbury.

Oh Crick (Fr) (h129 c147+) 6 ch.g Nikos – Other Crik (Fr) (Bigstone (Ire)) 2008/9 c19d* c16g^4 c16d^2 c20d^3 c20v^F c19s^2 c16d* c16g* Apr 2. Well, he's been amazing; he's just one of those horses that keeps doing it. He's never going to win by very far, so he probably just looked after his handicap mark for a bit, but I would imagine they'd be close to getting hold of him now if he hasn't improved again. It just took him a little time to get the hang of things over fences, but I was thrilled with him at Aintree (won Red Rum Chase); he travelled and jumped beautifully that day. He looks big and well and, as he's a young horse, there might just be a little bit more improvement to come. I'd like to think we might start him off in the Haldon Gold Cup (at Exeter).

Bensalem (Ire) (h146p F104) 6 b.g Turtle Island (Ire) – Peace Time Girl (Ire) (Buckskin (Fr)) 2008/9 F16s* 20d* 20d* 20v^2 21s* Apr 17. He's got huge potential. 'Choc' reckons he's one of the strongest horses he's ever sat on. He's won a point to point and he's going to go novice chasing. He might have one run over hurdles first to take the fizz out of him, the reason being I don't want him going charging down to the first fence fresh, not paying any attention. I've no doubt he'll get three miles, but I'll start him at two and a half miles—he's not slow. He's been beaten only once, and I think I'll get my revenge on Diamond Harry sooner rather than later; they split the width of the track the day they met and I think we could have done with a bit of company.

Nenuphar Collonges (Fr) (h– c146) 8 b.g Video Rock (Fr) – Diane Collonges (Fr) (El Badr) 2008/9 21d c24s* c29d c28v^6 c24d3 :: 2009/10 c25s^4 May 2. I always thought he would make into an out-and-out stayer, but I genuinely don't think he gets long distances, certainly on heavy ground. He ran two very good races at the end of last season, in the William Hill at Cheltenham and at Punchestown on ground that probably wasn't ideal carrying top weight. He's Hennessy-bound, but I'm not sure whether he will have a prep; he's got a very good record fresh and we might just go straight there. He seemed to gain confidence with his jumping last season and he's interesting; there could just be a big handicap in him, and I think decent ground suits him better than a bog.

Medermit (Fr) (h145) 5 gr.g Medaaly – Miss d'Hermite (Fr) (Solicitor (Fr)) 2008/9 17s* 17s^2 17s* 16d* 16d^2 16m^5 Apr 18. I think he was unlucky not to win the Supreme, but it was still a great run. He might have had enough by the time we got to the Scottish National meeting, and I certainly don't think he ran to his best. The plan is to go novice chasing but I might just give him a couple of runs over hurdles first; I'd quite like to look at the Greatwood at Cheltenham, and it might be we go straight there and he jumps fences after that. He's quite light, a typical French-bred, and he's never going to be a heavy-topped horse by any means, but he could be very interesting over fences. He's won on heavy, but he's a better horse on decent ground and I think we'll start him off over two miles; a stiff two miles is probably what he wants.

Bakbenscher (h135p) 6 gr.g Bob Back (USA) – Jessolle (Scallywag) 2008/9 16d* 16g 19s* 20g² Mar 7. He's potentially a very good horse, one of the best we've got. He's always been a bit gassy and can take a keen hold, but he got better as the season went on and just got hampered at the wrong stage in the EBF Final at Sandown. We always felt last year that he wouldn't be ready mentally for one of the big festivals, and therefore I didn't enter him, but ability-wise he's more than capable. We'll go novice chasing, but we'll just see how he shapes up in his schooling to see if we give him one run over hurdles or go straight over the big ones.

Miss Overdrive (F104) 5 b.m Overbury (Ire) – Free Travel (Royalty) 2008/9 F16g* F17d⁵ Apr 3. She's a full sister to Over Sixty who's done very well for us. I honestly thought she was ordinary last year—she was very backward and we only just got her on the track—but she won at Southwell and I think she excelled herself to be fifth at Aintree. She's done particularly well through the summer, strengthened, and she could easily do alright. I think the plan is to go one more run in a bumper before we go hurdling.

Chilli Rose (F100) 4 gr.f Classic Cliche (Ire) – Solo Rose (Roselier (Fr)) 2008/9 F16g* F17d⁶ Apr 3. I like them both, but I actually think she's even better than Miss Overdrive. I think she's very good, with huge potential. They both ran at Southwell and, when Miss Overdrive won, I thought Chilli Rose was a stone-bonking certainty in the second division because she was so far in front of her at home at the time. She hung at Aintree next time and we had to take a wolf tooth out afterwards, but she's fine now. She's stoutly bred, but has plenty of speed.

Timeform Betfair Racing Club

Ruby Kew 4 gr.f Great Palm – Park Jewel (Executive Perk) She hasn't run yet but has already been schooled over some telegraph pole logs and a few hurdles and was very good. We stepped her up last week to doing three canters twice a week, so we're very happy with her. She's got the size and scope to do everything in time. It'll be bumpers this season and we'll go on from there, but she could easily make into a chaser. She's got plenty of scope, a good attitude and did well during the summer.

TIMEFORM betfair
RACING CLUB

The Timeform Betfair Racing Club brings a new dimension to race club ownership. This unique and passionate club brings together the best Betfair and Timeform have to offer to make your race horse ownership experience the best there is. Membership includes:

- Free bet offers from Betfair
- 20% off all Timeform products at timeform.com/shop
- Breaking news and regular updates on all horses
- Dedicated club events & stable visits
- A free Timeform Race Card every day
- Horses in training with Alan King, Donald McCain Jnr, Tim Vaughan and Philip Hobbs

"You guys are actually bothered about the club and its members. A truly refreshing change."

FIND OUT MORE AT
TIMEFORMBETFAIRRACINGCLUB.COM
OR TEXT 'OWNER' & YOUR NAME TO 87474
Texts cost 10p plus your standard text rate.

Interview
Donald McCain

McCain Snr, or 'Ginger' as he's widely known, will forever be remembered for his exploits with the legendary three-time Grand National winner Red Rum, and son Donald is deservedly carving out a big reputation for himself as well. McCain Jnr's numbers have risen season on season since taking over the reins from his father in early-2006/7, and he's well on the way already to eclipsing last term's total of sixty-two wins, with thirteen on the board by the middle of September. Success at the Cheltenham Festival eluded Ginger during his long career, so it's even more impressive that Donald has put that record straight so soon, Cloudy Lane winning the Kim Muir at Prestbury Park in 2007 and Whiteoak the David Nicholson Mares' Hurdle the following year. McCain was one of the first choices to train for the Timeform Betfair Racing Club, and he wasted little time in justifying that choice as Marsool provided the club with their first winner over jumps at Newton Abbot in September. So here's to much more of the same for McCain, who generously took time recently to tell us about his team.

Cloudy Lane (c162) 9 b.g Cloudings (Ire) – Celtic Cygnet (Celtic Cone) 2008/9 c20s c24d^4 c25s^3 c24s* c22s^F c36d^{ur} Apr 4. He's in tremendous nick at the moment. We'll probably go to either the Charlie Hall or the Betfair and see how the season goes from there. We're not saying we won't go to Aintree again, but we maybe won't just target Aintree as we did last year. The frustration with the National was he was jumping twice as well as he'd jumped the year before and simply got racing a little bit going down to the Chair (where he unseated). I've always felt he maybe lacks a touch of class to be a top-notch chaser, but he's the sort in the big races you could certainly see running on to be third or fourth. Although he's won at

Cloudy Lane could be on his travels this winter

Haydock on heavy ground, he isn't as effective on it, so that might put us off going to Ireland, but we'll go wherever we have to go.

Whiteoak (Ire) (h146) 6 b.m Oscar (Ire) – Gayla Orchestra (Lord Gayle (USA)) 2008/9 16s² 16d 20d⁶ Apr 4. She obviously ran a screamer on her first run back last season; it'd been a hell of a long job and everyone in the yard deserves a lot of credit for getting her to Wincanton. We almost expected the next run, call it the 'bounce' factor, whatever you like, and then she's gone to Aintree and run with credit, sixth in the Aintree Hurdle. We have in the back of our minds she's better than that and was never really the same filly after Wincanton. She missed her chance to grow up the first part of last season and was chucked straight in against the best in the land in the Champion Hurdle, so hopefully she'll get her chance to run in some of the good races in the early part of this winter. We were toying giving her a run over three miles somewhere—she is bred to get a trip—and the only thing that puts you off is she's so quick.

Comhla Ri Coig (h143) 8 b.g Sir Harry Lewis (USA) – Analogical (Teenoso (USA)) 2008/9 22v³ 24s⁴ 20s* 16v* 16s² 24d² Apr 3. He's a smashing horse, we bred him and he just improved all last season. We ran him over all sorts of trips; we dropped

Whiteoak (noseband) will hopefully return to the form which saw her split Ashkazar and Punjabi (left) at Wincanton

him to two miles only because we'd get away with it on the ground some of the tracks were producing. For his age he hasn't had a lot of racing and I was thrilled with his second place in the Sefton at Aintree. He does seem to like being dropped in—he's a little bit nervous—and he just seems to relax back there. He'll go novice chasing subject to all the schooling going well, and it'll be an interesting winter.

Will Be Done (Ire) (c140) 8 ch.g Zaffaran (USA) – Deenish (Ire) (Callernish) 2008/9 c20s c24s³ c22s* c20s* c20d* c20s* c25s² Jan 31. He came at the start of last season having had next to no racing, just three runs in Ireland over fences, completing once. He grew all year, learnt his job with racing, and turned into a pretty smart novice and was quite unlucky to get beat at Wetherby the last day. We have the option of running him over hurdles, not to be clever but to get him some more experience before he gets thrown in against the good handicappers. He jumps and travels and goes on slow ground, but he's rated 148 by the BHA and we're under no illusions this season could be quite difficult.

Idle Talk (Ire) (c139) 10 br.g Hubbly Bubbly (USA) – Belon Breeze (Ire) (Strong Gale) 2008/9 c26s² c26v⁴ c24s c26m³ c36d Apr 4. Idle Talk deserves to win a race. I thought he'd won at Carlisle at the start of last season and, for a horse who was second in a SunAlliance, he probably didn't last home like you'd think. He tends to run well fresh and was unfortunate in the Becher Chase last year in that he's a decent ground horse and it was bottomless. He's jumped Aintree three or four times now and I'm sure we'll go back there.

Ernst Blofeld (Ire) (h129 F92) 5 br.g Flemensfirth (USA) – Estacado (Ire) (Dolphin Street (Fr)) 2008/9 F16v^3 20s* 20v^3 22v^2 20s* Mar 19. He's another one going novice chasing. He worked only okay at the start of last season, but when he went to the races he improved all the time. He's very immature, very babyish, but he looks every inch a chaser and is by a good stallion; he's definitely going to get a trip and jump fences.

Fiendish Flame (Ire) (h129 F90) 5 ch.g Beneficial – Deenish (Ire) (Callernish) 2008/9 F16g^5 17s^2 17v* 20v* 16d^3 20m^3 Apr 11. He'd be a good bit sharper than Ernst Blofeld mentally, but when he ran in his bumper at Cheltenham he came back and lost the plot completely; he was trying to run off with people and Adrian Lane, who rides him every day, did a lot of work on him. He still has his moments—the day he won at Uttoxeter he did everything to get himself beaten—but he grew up with racing and we learnt how to ride him. He settles better in front and his last run at Haydock was a blinding one. He's going novice chasing, and he'll stick at two and a half miles for the time being and see where we end up; I'm not saying he's going to be top class, but he could be quite smart.

Thumbs Up (h127p) 4 gr.g Intikhab (USA) – Exclusive Approval (USA) (With Approval (Can)) 2008/9 17s^3 16g^6 :: 2009/10 17g* 16s* May 15. I bought him off Luca Cumani and he was a mile-and-a-quarter horse basically on the Flat. It took a couple of runs to get him settled; it's not that the job's bothering him, it's just that he enjoys being out. He may settle better in a better race and, for a Flat horse, he doesn't look like he needs to be over hurdles for a long time; he has the look of one who'll take to a fence quite quickly, but we might leave it twelve months. He's still a novice over hurdles, so we'll be running him in a couple of the better novices early on, and later in the year we'll see about whether we go to Cheltenham or Aintree.

Son of Flicka (h125 F107) 5 b.g Groom Dancer (USA) – Calendula (Be My Guest (USA)) 2008/9 F17g^2 F17g^2 16d^2 17d^2 17s* 16d^2 20d^6 Feb 19. He came back with a knock after Huntingdon, a race which worked out funny. He's a grand horse with a great attitude and pedigree and, though he's not very big, he makes up for it with enthusiasm. He'll want two and a half miles and we will school him over fences. The owner's a local man, so Bangor's a possibility, and he might start in a handicap hurdle at the next Bangor meeting in October.

Fabalu (Ire) (h123p F105) 7 b.g Oscar (Ire) – Lizes Birthday (Ire) (Torus) 2008/9 F17s² 20v² 22s* 20s⁴ 24v* Feb 6. We maybe should have gone straight chasing with him last winter, but I thought we'd win our hurdle races first. He goes novice chasing this time around and he's a smashing horse; he stays and jumps and goes on soft ground. I'd like to think he could end up running in the four-miler at Cheltenham. He's not ground-dependent, but he does go in the mud and so many can't, so I'll sit and wait for the ground.

Glenwood Knight (Ire) (h116p F94) 6 ch.g Presenting – Glens Lady (Ire) (Mister Lord (USA)) 2008/9 F16v² 17s² Dec 5. He picked up a knock after he 'won' his novice hurdle at Exeter. He's a horse I think the world of, every inch a staying chaser with a staying chaser's pedigree being out of a half-sister to Papillon. He was second in his bumper, beaten by a nice horse, and he just ran a little green at Exeter and they took it off him. It might have been a blessing as we're still a novice, but the only thing that will stop him going chasing this season is lack of racecourse experience.

Alderley Rover (Ire) (h106p F89) 5 gr.g Beneficial – St Anne's Lady (Ire) (Roselier (Fr)) 2008/9 F16d³ 16g^F 19g^F 16s⁶ 16s³ 17g⁴ Mar 21. He's very babyish and got very lit up after his run at Doncaster; he's a Beneficial and they can just be a bit hot. It's taken a while to teach him his job, but he's a grand horse. He looks a chaser, but we'll probably spend another season over hurdles because he needs to grow up a bit and relax. He may well run in a handicap, and his mark looks potentially lenient; he was one of my nicer novices, in the same bunch as Comhla Ri Coig and Ernst Blofeld.

Alegralil (F109p) 4 b.f King's Theatre (Ire) – Lucy Glitters (Ardross) 2008/9 F17g* :: 2009/10 F17d* May 16. She's very good, we've thought that from day one. The one problem I had with her is I couldn't get weight off her; she was huge when she ran at Market Rasen. She's had a summer out and she has come down a little bit and I'm really happy with her. She's had a couple of schools, schooling nicely, and she could go right through the mares' system; she might not be quite as sharp and racy as Whiteoak, but at this stage she wouldn't have any less ability, either.

Wymott (Ire) (F100) 5 b.g Witness Box (USA) – Tanya Thyne (Ire) (Good Thyne (USA)) 2008/9 F16s² F17g* F17d Apr 4. He's back in full work. He's a very good-looking horse, a typical Trevor Hemmings one, and he'll go straight National Hunt novice hurdling and, hopefully, go through the system and win his races. We always like to have one for the Fixed-Brush series at Haydock and I don't see any reason why it wouldn't be him if he improves the way he was doing last year. He'll get two and a half miles, but he's a quality horse and I'm not sure he'll want three yet.

Timeform Betfair Racing Club

Marsool (h103p) 3 br.g Key of Luck (USA) – Chatifa (Ire) (Titus Livius (Fr)) 2009/10 17g² 17g* Sep 1. He hadn't shown a lot on the Flat, but I liked him straight away at the sales. He was grand (at Newton Abbot) and it was nice to see the horse who beat him first time bolt up at Stratford again. He's won one and I'd like to think he can win again, and it's his attitude that's pleasing me. I see him staying further and Jason (Maguire) thinks he'll be a better horse when they go a stronger gallop.

Interview
Tim Vaughan

Tim Vaughan could scarcely have made a more spectacular start to his training career. Having followed the path led by compatriots Peter Bowen, Evan Williams and Alison Thorpe, Vaughan is now firmly in the vanguard of this new wave of Welsh training success stories. A qualified chartered surveyor, Tim initially mixed this professional life with a highly fruitful career riding in point-to-points, and this side of the sport certainly hasn't been deserted as Vaughan's wife, Abbi, now trains a yard of pointers. On taking out a full training licence in November 2005, Tim has made astonishing progress. He really began to make his name in 2007/8, before outstripping anything achieved previously when saddling fifty-five winners in 2008/9, with the likes of Little Shilling, Helens Vision and Ski Sunday proving invaluable standard-bearers. However, the rate of progression at the Cowbridge yard has shown no sign at all of abating. Vaughan has made hay this summer and already has fifty wins on the board, comfortably more than any other trainer in Britain. With improved quality in the yard, the Vaughans can certainly be expecting to be feeding at the top table come the end of 2009/10. Tim has shown a rare aptitude for improving those he inherits, and is a regular sight at the various Horses In Training sales, so it made perfect sense for him to train Another Brother for the Timeform Betfair Racing Club.

Atouchbetweenacara (Ire) (c150p) 8 b.g Lord Americo – Rosie Lil (Ire) (Roselier (Fr)) 2008/9 c20d^2 c24g^F c24s^2 c21d* Apr 15. He's lovely, looks the business and was very progressive for Venetia Williams last season. Hopefully he could just be the real deal. He's the most exciting horse in my yard, there's no question about it. We'll try and aim him at the Paddy Power, but we only got him in a couple of weeks ago and it'll be a bit of a race against time. If we can't get him there he'll probably go to the Grand Sefton at Aintree. I'll be happy to go there because of

Stan is one of several Paul Beck-owned horses to have moved from Venetia Williams to Tim Vaughan this summer

the way he jumped round Cheltenham last season; if he goes like that at Aintree he'll have the hairs standing up on the back of my neck! These are just the types I need right now. If all goes well, we'll be there on the Saturday afternoons competing with the big boys, and that's where I want to be.

Stan (NZ) (c150) 10 b.g Super Imposing (NZ) – Take Care (NZ) (Wham (Aus)) 2008/9 c17g^2 c20s^{pu} c16d^5 c21d* c21v^{pu} c24g c20g^4 c21d^{pu} c36d^F **Apr 4.** Another new recruit. We'll run him in the big staying chases. He's rated 148 by the BHA—they've dropped him 6 lb since he ran in the National—and he's a bit more exposed. He won off 143 at Cheltenham on New Year's Day, a £31,000 race, so it's not impossible that he'll start off in the Paddy Power as well. Last year he started at Ascot where he finished second to Bleu Superbe and we could look at that, though I think he wants a bit further now.

Flintoff (USA) (c137§) 8 ch.g Diesis – Sahibah (USA) (Deputy Minister (Can)) 2008/9 c27s^5 c33s^2 **Mar 14.** He runs his best races at the likes of Uttoxeter, he was second in the Midlands National in March, and we'll be looking at those sort of races, the likes of the Eider. He wears blinkers and, having been with Venetia Williams for a few years, he's the sort that a change of scenery could do a whole lot of good for. He's an out-and-out slogger and the Scottish National could be his day. Though, even the Grand National couldn't be out of the question, especially if it came up soft.

War of The World (Ire) (h97+ c134) 7 b.g Shernazar – Fairpark (Ire) (Shardari) 2008/9 c24d^2 c22g^5 c22g c25d^5 :: 2009/10 c25f c22s^2 c23m* Sep 5. I was delighted after he won at Stratford the other day. £18,000 looks very cheap now, doesn't it? He doesn't carry a lot of condition, but hopefully we've sweetened him up and he's had a different style of training as well as a change of scenery. He won nicely. Richard Johnson said he was just in front for long enough and he was idling; the handicapper put him up 7 lb for that and, though he went down to Valley Ride at Market Rasen next time, I still don't think we've got to the bottom of him. He stays well and he could even be a Welsh National type. Of course, he's a novice over hurdles, too, so I've still got that up my sleeve as well.

Little Shilling (Ire) (h125 c110p) 7 ch.g Bob's Return (Ire) – Minouette (Ire) (Beau Sher) 2008/9 c24m^5 c22g^5 c24m^5 22g^4 20s* 24s* 24m* 23s* c26s* 27s* 20d :: 2009/10 24d^4 24m* Sep 11. He's progressed massively and will be aimed at the three-mile plus handicap hurdles and chases. Not many see out three and a half miles really well and that's one thing he's got in his favour. I still think 125 is a winnable mark and he likes good ground. So when everyone else is swerving decent ground in the winter he'll be out.

Rupestrian (h120) 3 b.g Fantastic Light (USA) – Upper Strata (Shirley Heights) 2009/10 16m* 16d* 17m* 17d* 16m^2 Aug 20. He's been a great horse over the summer for us. Wants cut in the ground: he got run off his feet last time when beaten by Royal Max, he was flat out, and I just thought he'd been on the go for long enough. We've given him a break now until December and we'll bring him back for the Fred Winter, straight to Cheltenham first time out probably. If he runs well in that, we'll look to go to Aintree for the 4-y-o juvenile hurdle, the same route that Ski Sunday went down. He wants two and a half, three miles longer term.

Manor Park (Ire) (h115) 4 b.g Hernando (Fr) – Campiglia (Ire) (Fairy King (USA)) 2008/9 16v^2 16d 16s^2 16s^4 16g^2 16g^6 :: 2009/10 16s Apr 29. I like him, he's a really nice type of horse. We've given him a wind operation and he'll start off in about four weeks time. He'll have a hurdles campaign this season, put him away over the summer and come back chasing next season.

Unforgettable (Ire) (h113 c113) 6 b.g Norwich – Miss Lulu (Ire) (King Luthier) 2008/9 16g* 16g^4 20s^{pu} 20g 16m^4 16s^6 16g^2 :: 2009/10 19g^4 19g^5 19m c21g^F c20m^3 Aug 31. He finished third the other day on his first run for us. Richard got off him and said he'd probably be best rolling along from the front over a strong two miles with cut in the ground. We'll just keep him novice chasing now unless a nice hurdle pops up that we fancy taking our chances at.

Arctic Shadow (h112 c112) 7 b.g Bonny Scot (Ire) – Dickies Girl (Saxon Farm) 2008/9 21g⁴ 24s 25g⁵ 24v³ 24d^F 24s⁵ 20s 25s :: 2009/10 c19s² c24g c24d* c22d* 24g* 27v² **Aug 4.** Lovely horse, honest, genuine, wants mud up to his eyeballs and he stays forever. He's having a little break now but we'll most probably aim him for the Lincolnshire National at Market Rasen on Boxing Day. He'd been on the go for a year and then he came to us: we screwed him to the boards and won three with him. I think he'll definitely win another race from his current mark.

Baily Storm (Ire) (h103p) 7 br.g Anshan – Euroblend (Ire) (The Parson) 2008/9 16s 20v 24g 19d^pu :: 2009/10 20g 24s⁵ 22g² 20s^pu **Jul 29.** I thought he was one who would do well for coming over here. He looked a bit wrong in his coat when he joined us but he's improved massively now and looked good when making a winning start for us in a maiden hurdle at Stratford in mid-September, the front two finishing miles clear. His best form is on good to firm ground. He'll jump a fence as well. He's not a great horse, but he'll pick up his lower grade races.

Danimix (Ire) (h–p F91) 4 b.g Dr Massini (Ire) – Spring Blend (Ire) (Persian Mews) 2008/9 NR :: 2009/10 F16m* F16d⁵ F17m² 16m⁶ **Sep 6.** He's only a four-year-old and is having a bit of a break now. Looks nice, I think he'll handle most ground and we'll bring him back for a maiden or novice hurdle at the back end of the winter season. He definitely wants further and I think he's a lovely staying chaser in the making.

Timeform Betfair Racing Club

Another Brother (Ire) (h124 c95p) 7 b.g Supreme Leader – Sister Rosza (Ire) (Roselier (Fr)) 2008/9 22s* 24g² c24s⁴ 24d² 20d⁶ 22d^F **Mar 14.** He's had a wind operation since he joined us and is doing all the right things. He's been back in work for about six weeks. I saw him win in October last year and he absolutely bolted in that day. That was just a novice hurdle but they gave him a mark of 117 for that. They said he blundered a few times when he went chasing, but he's a strong sort and we'll get him over fences no problem. So the plan is to win a nice handicap hurdle on a Saturday before going back over fences. He's just been popping over hurdles and poles every Tuesday and Friday and he's as sweet as a nut.

Future Stars

Rebecca Curtis

If there isn't already, there'll soon start to be some serious pressure attached to training jumpers in Wales bearing in mind the success stables in that part of the British Isles have enjoyed in recent seasons. Peter Bowen led the way, followed not long after by Evan Williams and Alison Thorpe, and Tim Vaughan has arguably taken the mantle to an even greater level with some staggering success during the last two campaigns. Rebecca Curtis will do well to emulate that quartet when it comes to revitalising apparently lost causes and improving those seemingly exposed with other yards, but she's certainly made a good fist of it with limited ammunition and Timeform very much expects more of the same in the remainder of 2009/10.

Traditionally, the summer has been an especially lucrative time of the year for Welsh handlers—Vaughan is currently eight winners clear of his nearest pursuer in the trainers' table and Williams only two places behind—though, interestingly, of Curtis' fifteen winners to date only three have come in the summer months, suggesting she's already starting to make the transition it's taken her predecessors a little longer to achieve.

The versatile Mango Catcher was the early flag-bearer for the yard, providing Curtis with her first two winners as he improved plenty for joining the stable (formerly with Paul Nolan), and now in dual bumper winner The Jigsaw Man she has a horse with the potential to take her operation on to a higher level. Curtis' career as a fully-fledged trainer is little over eighteen months and a hundred runners old, and these very early signs point to her having all the attributes required to think she's a handler going places.

Trainer's View: I was brought up showjumping mainly. I was in the Welsh team as a junior and quite successful doing that. I went on to work for Peter Bowen for two years, which was a good grounding, and then started point-to-pointing, riding myself for a season. After that, I went to America for four years working as assistant trainer to Dan Hendricks. That was that really, and I came back and got the licence out then in March 2008.

We've got only twenty-two boxes, but we're just putting more up and hopefully we'll have twenty-five, thirty for the winter. We've got twenty in at the moment and we should have a few more over the next couple of months and I'm really pleased with how things have been going. It should be a better winter as we've got some nice younger horses, when previously we've been working with older handicappers from Ireland; we've just got a better quality now.

I've been really pleased with our bumper horses in particular, most we've run have won or been placed. Myself and Gearoid Costello, the nephew of Tom Costello, have bought a few together at the sales which we'll bring on and hopefully sell to owners if we can. A lot of them we do own together, or I own myself, so it'd be nice if they showed some promise if we could get them to more owners.

This season I just want to have more winners and get some good quality younger horses out. I'd rather quality over quantity for the time being. I hope also we've got some nice novices who can run in some better races, especially The Jigsaw Man; Donal Devereaux rode him and said he's the best horse he's ever sat on, just how he quickens off the pace he goes at. The two bumpers he's won have been on the bridle, so you'd hope he could be a Cheltenham novice hurdler. The horse who beat him at Galway (Loosen My Load, see p48) is a proper horse, yet I think on a flatter track we might have reversed places. As for jockeys, I'd always use

	NHF	Juveniles	Hurdlers	Chasers	All
Win prize money (£)					
2007/8				3,903	3,903
2008/9	1,918		16,881	5,855	24,654
Cumulative	1,918		16,881	9,758	28,557
Winners-Horses					
2007/8			0-2	1-1	1-3
2008/9	1-4		4-7	1-5	6-13
Cumulative	1-4		4-8	2-5	6-14
Wins-Runs					
2007/8			0-3	1-3	1-6
2008/9	1-6		5-37	2-24	8-67
Cumulative	1-6		5-40	3-27	9-73
Strike Rate (%)					
2007/8			0	33	17
2008/9	17		14	8	12
Cumulative	17		13	11	12
Profit / Loss (£1)					
2007/8			-3.00	.50	-2.50
2008/9	-2.25		-7.62	-17.33	-27.20
Cumulative	-2.25		-10.62	-16.83	-29.70
Median Rating					
2007/8			71	114	87
2008/9	84		99	105	100
Cumulative	84		92	110	99

A P McCoy on our novices if we could get him, but obviously Jonjo usually has runners in those better races and we'll just go with the best we can get.

Horse To Follow: Gus Macrae, who finished second in a twenty-four-runner bumper at Fairyhouse (for Tony Mullins). He's definitely improved for a break—we gave him three months off—and we're excited about him. We'll probably run him in the Cheltenham bumper in October and then he'll go novice hurdling. He's by Accordion, from the same family as Buck House.

Paul Flynn

Paul Flynn carved out a relatively successful time as a jumps rider, particularly during his time spent as understudy to Richard Johnson at Philip Hobbs's yard, and the early evidence points to his training career being even more lucrative.

There were nine months between Flynn's first runner in April 2007 and his first winner (both Bronte Bay, incidentally), but during the same length of time from January 2009 he's already had fifteen, twelve of which have come over obstacles. His level-stakes profit is currently over £120, a staggering number even if the 66/1-success of Keogh's Tradbar at Uttoxeter skews the figures somewhat.

Flynn has wisely followed a path carved most notably by Gordon Elliott in recent times, shrewdly targeting races all over Britain to find opportunities, though he's had plenty of success in his homeland as well and is set fair to continue to do so. Archie Boy and Kalellshan have been the main contributors to his impressive 2009/10 tally, and, with the more competitive jumps action on the horizon, it's sure to help the rise of Flynn's stock that both are useful and up to taking their chance in better company.

Trainer's View: It's going well, the horses are doing grand. It's been a bit of a nightmare in Ireland with the weather, but it's the same for everyone I suppose and that's one of the reasons we go to England as much as we do. It obviously gives you encouragement when you see the likes of Gordon (Elliott) doing well, but I was there for a long time as well riding with Philip Hobbs and he was great at finding races; it's about running in the right ones and giving them their best chance. I think that's my strength, I suppose, is doing that. It's very hard to place horses in Ireland and in Britain you'll go over and be thinking there's only one or two who can beat you. You can definitely say the racing in Ireland is more competitive; with a lot of horses we bring, people say they're well handicapped, but they couldn't win in Ireland off their Irish marks, which are sometimes 10 lb lower, perhaps more. The ground in Britain is another major factor; they run on soft all summer, bring them to England for good ground, and it's bound to bring out improvement from them if they're the conditions they've been wanting.

Originally, I came right from Hobbs's to ride back in Ireland, but got a bad injury and then started doing some pre-training. I went in on my own straight away, I was never assistant to anyone or anything. I love the day-to-day involvement of it and it's a lot more rewarding when they win, but there's plenty more people here other than me.

We've got twenty horses at the moment and I'm happy to stay around that number, for the time being anyway. We could put another twenty in if we wanted, but by having less numbers I think it's easier to keep the good horses and get rid of bad ones. We've got some good ones in. Archie Boy has already won four races, and Kalellshan will go to Cheltenham for the novice race in October. Kalellshan is probably better right-handed, but it's hard to find races going that way in Britain,

	NHF	Juveniles	Hurdlers	Chasers	All
Win prize money (£)					
2006/7			5,679		5,679
2007/8			8,790		8,790
2008/9	5,398	7,087	4,662	7,404	24,551
Cumulative	5,398	7,087	19,131	7,404	39,020
Winners-Horses					
2006/7	0-0		0-0		0-0
2007/8	0-0		1-2		1-2
2008/9	0-0	0-0	0-0	0-0	0-0
Cumulative	0-0	0-0	1-2	0-0	1-2
Wins-Runs					
2006/7	0-2		1-1		1-3
2007/8	0-12		2-33		2-45
2008/9	1-12	1-3	1-55	1-21	4-91
Cumulative	1-26	1-3	4-89	1-21	7-139
Strike Rate (%)					
2006/7	0		100		33
2007/8	0		6		4
2008/9	8	33	2	5	4
Cumulative	4	33	4	5	5
Profit / Loss (£1)					
2006/7	-2.00		.00		-2.00
2007/8	-12.00		-27.67		-39.67
2008/9	-11.00	-2.00	-54.00	-20.00	-87.00
Cumulative	-25.00	-2.00	-81.67	-20.00	-128.67
Median Rating					
2006/7					
2007/8			113		113
2008/9					
Cumulative			113		113

and a stiff two miles will really suit him. A P McCoy rode Archie Boy at Ffos Las and we always try to get him when we come over. I like Jason Maguire, too, he's a very good rider.

I'll probably have only a handful of horses for the winter, because most of mine want good ground, so the main aim long term is to look for more winter types. In the short term, we're just trying to get as many winners as we can during the summer. I don't set any targets as such, I just hope the horses continue to run well and win as many as they can.

Horse To Follow: If you follow **Keogh's Bar** this season you won't go too far wrong. I shouldn't have run him at Newton Abbot (fell), but I'll drop him to two and a half miles and he's a horse that will progress next year; he wants good ground, and should make into a nice staying horse.

Andy Haynes

Late developer, slow burner, call it whatever you will, but Andy Haynes has certainly made much more of an impact in the training ranks as his career has gone on, especially in the National Hunt sphere. Granted, Haynes has been going since only 2004, but jumps winners have increased healthily by the season and his eye-catching progress at the start of 2009/10 very much marks him down as a young trainer on the up.

Haynes had seven winners from sixty-nine runners last season, a decent enough strike-rate of 10% resulting in a very minor level-stakes loss, yet already this campaign he's more than doubled his number of winners, with fifteen to his name before the middle of September. Naturally, his strike-rate has improved, to a very impressive 25% in fact, but his level-stake profit of almost £35 is arguably even more noteworthy.

It's Haynes's handling of previously quirky types that has really impressed, not dissimilar in fact to another perennially underrated handler, Richard Lee. Haynes has revitalised Stumped, Heir To Be and Willies Way in no uncertain terms, all of whom appeared to have lost the plot prior to joining him, and it seems particularly significant when there's money for his runners; Heir To Be, for example, was the subject of a huge gamble prior to winning at Folkestone in 2008/9. It's surely only a matter of time before Haynes's skills are rewarded with increased patronage and, if that does indeed prove the case, he'll surely remain in the ascendant during the remainder of 2009/10 and beyond.

Trainer's View: I'm delighted with how things are going. Four and a half years ago we bought four horses at Ascot Sales for a total of £8,000, with no owners, and today we've got seventy plus in and we've had over fifty winners this calendar year. Harry Findlay's backing us now, Roger Brookhouse is a new owner, Graham and Di Robinson, who bred Overdose, are here as well.

We're very lucky that we train in five-star accomodation and that we've got 360 acres of paddock, which allows me to turn the older horses out, something we do a lot here. It might not work for everyone, but results show it works for us. We've had Heir To Be and Come Out Firing, who've both won five this year, and we bought L'Eau du Nil out of a seller and he won a £13,000 handicap hurdle. I'm looking all the time for more, and I've always got orders in for any I buy.

We had no more than six jumpers here not long ago, before we went to the Doncaster Sales in 2007 to buy a nice Flat horse to go jumping; that was Border Castle, who won the Scottish Champion Hurdle the next April, and then of course all your others owners think 'I wouldn't mind a jumper' and it went from there.

In the early days I worked at Jack Holt's and Richard Hannon's—I was at Richard's a long time—and I've picked up bits from both and put in my own things that I like to do and it's all worked well. I started out the back of Richard Hannon's yard

	NHF	Juveniles	Hurdlers	Chasers	All
Win prize money (£)					
2007/8			60,884	9,759	70,643
2008/9			22,316	12,913	35,229
Cumulative			83,200	22,672	105,872
Winners-Horses					
2007/8	0-2	0-1	1-5	1-2	2-9
2008/9	0-1		3-12	1-5	4-16
Cumulative	0-3	0-1	4-14	1-5	5-21
Wins-Runs					
2007/8	0-4	0-1	2-12	2-10	4-27
2008/9	0-1		5-48	2-20	7-69
Cumulative	0-5	0-1	7-60	4-30	11-96
Strike Rate (%)					
2007/8	0	0	17	20	15
2008/9	0		10	10	10
Cumulative	0	0	12	13	11
Profit / Loss (£1)					
2007/8	-4.00	-1.00	41.00	19.00	55.00
2008/9	-1.00		.75	-2.00	-2.25
Cumulative	-5.00	-1.00	41.75	17.00	52.75
Median Rating					
2007/8	68	–	–	109	88
2008/9	–		–	95	91
Cumulative	–	–	–	95	90

in a little barn with twenty-four boxes and one paddock, but when we got the numbers up in about 2004 we decided to find somewhere we could expand to and, with pot luck, we stumbled upon where we are now.

I'm ambitious—I live and breathe horses—and just want more winners, which we've managed to do every year so far.

Horse To Follow: I would go for a new horse we've bought, **My Turn Now**, who was a very good hurdler in his day. He's one of those that lost his way, but if we could get him back to that sort of form he must be one to follow.

Harry Haynes

A recent link-up with upwardly-mobile Scottish trainer James Ewart could prove the making of the already promising Northern conditional Harry Haynes. So many young riders struggle as the end of their claim approaches and then expires, but the association with Ewart, who himself enjoyed his best season by some way in 2008/9 with twelve winners, almost double his previous best, should ensure Haynes gets the support that's so vital when it comes to a jockey making his presence felt in the professional ranks. There's likely to be some time before that happens, however, and in the meantime, punters can take advantage of Haynes's claim; he rides like a fully-fledged jockey, and the importance of his 5 lb allowance really can't be overstated.

Haynes first caught the eye during his time with Nicky Richards, though not with one of Richards' inmates. Instead, Haynes forged a successful partnership with prolific pointer/hunter chaser Natiain, winning three times within three weeks and impressing with how well he got the headstrong front runner settled and jumping. Natiain's trainer Alistair Crow, another underrated handler from north of the border, provided Haynes with his final winner of 2008/9 courtesy of Ayr bumper winner Carters Rest, and he's sure to be one to look forward to in novice hurdles for Haynes this season, as is Turbo Island, who was two from two in that sphere for Ewart.

Statistics-wise, Haynes continued on the up last season, even if his strike-rate went down. Fourteen winners was an increase of three on his total the campaign before, and the fact Haynes improved his number of rides markedly at the same time, riding almost three times as many as he had in 2007/8 suggests plenty of others have taken note of his ability.

Weight should never be a problem with Haynes, either. At present he's more than able to ride at 10-0, yet his lack of weight is in no way a sign of lack of strength; he's not only a polished, tidy rider, but a strong one, too, as his narrow win aboard Sa Suffit at Catterick in early-2009 very much showed. Here's hoping there are many more in 2009/10, and all the evidence points to that indeed proving the case so long as he stays injury-free.

Peter Toole

It's almost taken for granted that jockeys will record a hefty level-stakes loss during the course of a season, such are the strike-rates usually involved in terms of winners to rides, especially for young riders just making their way in the sport. Often, conditionals and amateurs take rides on runners with little chance as they seek to gain experience; trainers naturally have to develop trust in the riders' skills, so it's very rare they'll risk an inexperienced jockey on something in their care with good claims on form in a race. So far, though, 7-lb conditional Peter Toole has been an exception in his season and a bit as a jumps rider, accumulating a mere £8 loss in his first season and, in little over the four months of the latest one, racking up a level-stakes profit in excess of £70.

There are also reasons beyond statistics to believe Toole's future is very bright indeed. He's certainly sound tactically, just as comfortable riding one forcefully (note Pure Magic at Newton Abbot) as he is coming from off the pace (Stumped at Market Rasen), and he's capable of riding at 10-0 as well.

Charlie Mann's likely influence can't be underestimated, either. Dave Crosse was brought along steadily, and with good effect, by the trainer, but it is Mann's work alongside retained rider Noel Fehily that really marks him down as a good mentor, providing a large bulk of the rider's forty-two winners in his season as champion conditional in 2000/01. In keeping with that, Toole has had most of his rides, and winners, for Mann. Three of Toole's eight wins as an amateur were provided by Mann and, since entering the professional ranks, Toole has added another nine successes to his collection, numbering horses trained by up-and-coming pair Alex Hales and Andy Haynes amongst them. It's clear therefore that Toole's skills haven't been noticed by Timeform alone, but he's still enough of an unknown quantity to suggest his presence alongside a horse's name won't shorten the price artificially.

Horses of Interest From The Sales

National Hunt Chase winner Tricky Trickster prompted some fierce bidding when sent under the hammer

The current economic climate might have been expected to impact greatly on recent National Hunt 'Horses In Training' sales, but the figures suggest the downturn is less significant than first feared, at the top end at least. Doncaster's spring sales remained fairly strong, with **Tricky Trickster**, a near-selection for this season's 'Fifty', topping the sales list when joining Paul Nicholls for £320,000. Tricky Trickster has Grand National type written all over him, so it was no surprise to hear his new trainer nominate the Aintree spectacular as his main target. Last season, his first outside points, was a very productive one for Tricky Trickster, culminating in a dominant wide-margin win upped to four miles in the National Hunt Chase at the Cheltenham Festival. Pre-Aintree, Tricky Trickster is set to revert to hurdling and, whilst he's always going to be better over fences given his physique and bold jumping, maiden and novice company over hurdles is likely to provide some pretty easy pickings until the Aintree weights are released. Watch out also for **Apartman**, who was also sold to join Nicholls, this time from Alistair Charlton. Many will view Apartman's big-priced success against some vaunted rivals in a good Ayr juvenile to end last season as a fluke, but the time compared favourably with the Scottish Champion Hurdle run later in the afternoon and he certainly shouldn't be underestimated whichever path his new connections choose to take; ideally, that path will be chasing, as Apartman is a very imposing type physically and will be able to utilise the ever-handy four-year-old allowance.

Tricky Trickster's sale was a product of the Million In Mind Partnership's annual dispersal sale, but one owner whose activity at Doncaster didn't seem entirely planned was Trevor Hemmings', a major sufferer during the ongoing uncertainty courtesy of his heavy involvement in the leisure industry. Hemmings sent plenty to Doncaster in a bid to reduce his string and focus even more on quality than quantity, and leading the way amongst those he parted with could well be **Another Brother**, who was knocked down to join Tim Vaughan for a good deal less than was probably expected at £18,000. Another Brother made good progress over hurdles for Jonjo O'Neill in 2008/9, winning a Uttoxeter novice and chasing home the rampant Heathcliff in a handicap at Chepstow, and he's just the type to show even better form over fences bearing in mind his size and free-going demeanour. Securing good deals and improving his new arrivals has been the meat and drink of Vaughan's rapid rise to prominence in the training ranks, and there are several others recent purchases besides Another Brother who can be expected to make their presence felt for the stable in 2009/10. **Master Charm** heads the list having been bought out of Carl Llewellyn's stable. Llewellyn, who has since quit training to rejoin team Twiston-Davies, had a disappointing season by his standards prior to Hennessy's win in the bet365 Gold Cup at Sandown, and the lightly-raced Master Charm was one of his inmates who left the impression he's better than his results suggested. Master Charm is a good-looking half-brother to fairly useful chaser Antonius Caesar, and there's been more than enough in his runs over both hurdles and fences to believe the best of him has yet to be seen. **Gobejolly** and **Etoile d'Or** have also joined the Vaughan bandwagon, from Ben Case and Matt Gingell respectively. Neither trainer have boasted high strike-rates in recent seasons (the latter has since been banned for two years for administering a 'milkshake'), and their former inmates both often shaped as if possessing more ability than a cursory glance at their form figures would indicate. Both are strong-travelling types and figure on basement marks, while Etoile d'Or was of a much better standard on the Flat than she's shown so far over hurdles and Gobejolly the same with regards bumpers.

Another Welshman whose record with cheap purchases bears close inspection is Evan Williams; note in recent times the likes of State of Play, Winter Star and William Butler. Emulating that trio will take some doing, but **Jamestown Bay** catches the eye after joining Williams from Owen Brennan, a trainer who has had only three winners over jumps since 2006; ironically, the last of those was Jamestown Bay, at Market Rasen in March 2008. The seven-year-old showed better form in defeat after, chasing home Ouzbeck, Qulinton and The Vicar at the track on his final outing, and he's yet to have his stamina tested fully, something Williams will no doubt be keen to exploit in handicap hurdles this season.

Martin Hill is less of a household name than Messrs Nicholls, Vaughan and Williams, but his work with the much-improved ex-Henrietta Knight trained Bally Conn certainly caught *Timeform*'s eye in 2008/9 and new acquisition **Porta Vogie** could be the type to make similar progress this season. Porta Vogie was well backed more than once for Ian Williams and often shaped better than the result suggests, including, funnily enough, when third to Bally Conn in a Kempton novice handicap in February.

Despite increased focus, stable changes still aren't given the coverage they warrant, ensuring plenty still start at bigger odds than they should, and the list above will hopefully go a long way to proving the point in 2009/10.

Tote 'Ten To Follow' Competition

The annual selection of ten horses for the Tote/Racing Post Ten To Follow competition provides as clear a sign as any that the dawn of the National Hunt season 'proper' is upon us. The thought of cheering one's entry ever higher up the leaderboard is enough to ward off cold winter evenings, compulsory Christmas shopping treks and the nonentity of a month that is February. The only blessing that arrives with the knowledge that all hope of winning the damn thing has long gone is that it's March by then, and Cheltenham is just days away. Nonetheless, just as rituals are passed down through communities and religions, largely for symbolic purpose, we must pick the ten horses that, on entering, we know with a fair degree of certainty will lead us to a fair chunk of the £1 million guaranteed prize fund. Having selected fifty to follow in the main section of this publication, it may seem logical simply to cherry-pick from those horses. However, doing so would not play to the demands of the competition. Whilst the winners of the fifteen all-important bonus races rack up the top points, it will always be the best horses who provide the backbone of any successful entry. To reinforce the point, a look at Sam Hoskins' winning entry from 2008/9 shows us that Madison du Berlais, Big Buck's, Imperial Commander, Kauto Star, Master Minded and Punjabi provided him with the bulk of his score, whereas those drawn into the 'Fifty' are, naturally, far less established and won't be competing at quite such an exalted level in the main, for the time being at least!

Kauto Star has been an automatic selection in this competition for several seasons now and, for many he will be again, the best horse in training as he is. However, Paul Nicholls and his team last season came to the conclusion that as he advances in age Kauto Star's career will be best preserved with the 'cotton wool treatment', meaning we are most unlikely to see him more than twice before he bids to retain his crown in the Cheltenham Gold Cup. Admittedly, one of those outings will surely come in another bonus race, the Stan James King George VI Chase, a contest he's won in spectacular fashion for the past three seasons, but the other is most likely to be in the JNwine.com Champion Chase at Down Royal, a race which falls before the start of the competition. As such Kauto Star's maximum score is likely to be the 100pts he managed last term. If that was a guaranteed return then it's not to be sniffed at, but there are reasons for thinking that it may be advisable to oppose the majority and give the great horse the swerve as he rises ten.

One Paul Nicholls-trained Champion who needs including, however, is **Big Buck's**. He proved a revelation on reverting to timber last season, emerging as the best stayer around, and he'll take plenty of beating in all such races this season as well. In addition to that, he also remains a plausible points earner over fences, in which sphere his true potential has yet to be fulfilled. Another of the Ditcheat battalion who'll secure his fair share of points is, of course, **Master Minded**. Despite winning four from four before heading off on his summer holiday, Master Minded seemed to have more doubters than at the end of 2007/8, a somewhat less impressive display at Cheltenham followed by a hard-fought victory over Big Zeb at Punchestown leading many to query the precise nature of his ability. Either way, there can be no

That top-notch two-miler Master Minded promises to be a popular choice again

questioning the fact the six-year-old is head and shoulders above his contemporaries in the two-mile division and, with none of the novices from last season appealing as likely threats in the division, he looks nailed on to be one of the leading points scorers.

Tom George enjoyed a fantastic season with his exuberant grey **Nacarat** last season, and his development into a high-class chaser incorporated a thrilling success in the Racing Post Chase at Kempton. Whilst he was subsequently found out against the very best when third to Voy Por Ustedes at Aintree, his rise through the ranks possibly hasn't plateaued, so he may yet prove competitive in the top races, not least the King George on Boxing Day given how well he took to the course last term. With such prestigious races likely to be his target throughout the campaign, Nacarat can be expected to pick up his fair share of points.

Second-season novice Imperial Commander proved a massive hit with those who selected him in 2008/9, successful in two of the bonus races and duly racking up 114 points. He can't be expected to achieve as much this time round, however, and the difficult part is trying to pinpoint a horse with a similar profile who may be able to emulate him. **Atouchbetweenacara** is, admittedly, not about to embark on his second season chasing, rather his third, but he remains relatively lightly-raced and appeals as one who can win a big handicap before making the leap to Graded company. As Tim Vaughan pointed out, however, it's something of a race against time to have him ready for Cheltenham, though if the signs are positive just ahead of the entry deadline he could well be one to have on side; he's the one with the dubious honour of featuring in both this piece and the Fifty', so let's just hope he's up to handling such pressure! **Duc de Regniere**'s form took off over hurdles last term when he progressed into one of the best stayers around, though it mustn't be forgotten that he'd shown an aptitude for chasing in three starts the season before and, having had his limitations exposed somewhat at the very highest level over timber, Nicky Henderson will presumably be looking at handicap chases for him now. He appeals as just the sort that can be placed to advantage in valuable contests, versatile regarding distance requirements (effective from two and a half miles to twenty-five furlongs), and having looked a proficient enough jumper in three previous tries over fences. **Killyglen**'s novice season finished with a flourish when he took the Grade 2 at the Grand National meeting and valuable staying handicaps, first and foremost the Hennessy, will surely be on the agenda for him in 2009/10. He will have to improve again from his initial handicap mark of 153, but that's all he did during the course of his novice campaign and he still hasn't had all that much racing, so Howard Johnson certainly has something to play with. Whether or not Killyglen has it in him to make the leap to the elite level is perhaps open to some question, but he should at least put himself in a position to take in some of the valuable Nationals further down the line. Another stayer who could be worth chancing is the impressive Cheltenham Foxhunters' winner **Cappa Bleu**. The seven-year-old came from the pointing field with a massive reputation, and the manner in which he justified it on what was his hunter debut was of one with a very bright future. He sports the colours of 2006 Hennessy winner State of Play and, like that one, he's to be trained by Evan Williams as he ventures into the professional ranks. He'll need to take another considerable step forward if he's to prove competitive with the 'big boys', but that's far from inconceivable given how exciting a prospect he looked when galloping relentlessly up the Cheltenham hill in March.

Speaking of Nationals, and most specifically the Aintree one, it's worth pointing out that including the winner of the great race isn't crucial to your chances in the Ten To Follow. In two of the last three years, the winner of the race hasn't even been included in the list of five hundred from which selections must be made—namely Silver Birch and Mon Mome—and a safer ploy is probably to draft in a Natinal fancy during the transfer window. **Big Fella Thanks** and **Tricky Trickster** are two who make some appeal at this very early stage, but with both of Nicholls' charges likely to be trained specifically for the race, it is doubtful that they'll be racking up many points before Aintree.

With Punchestowns set to try his hand over fences this season, the biggest danger to Big Buck's dominance as a staying hurdler is once more likely to be Kasbah Bliss—unless, as was mooted earlier, Nicholls opts to send his charge back over the larger obstacles. As was the case in 2008, Kasbah Bliss has had quite an extensive (and successful) Flat campaign, something which saw him restricted to just two runs over hurdles in 2008/9. Similar can be expected this time around and, as such, he's probably one to be wary of from a points-scoring perspective. Depending on how Willie Mullins opts to play his hand, it could well be that any threat to Big Buck's will emerge from County Carlow. In **Mikael d'Haguenet** and **Fiveforthree** he trains two top-class prospects who are more than capable of making their mark at the highest level over hurdles or fences. The question is, will they be kept apart? However things pan out, both certainly warrant consideration for inclusion given they'll more than likely be winning many more races than they lose, the only doubt with the latter being that he hasn't stood much racing in the past couple of seasons.

Fiveforthree is likely to be one of the highest-rated hurdlers going chasing in 2009/10

The two-mile division seems rather more straightforward, however. Those looking to include the Champion Hurdler appear to have a straight choice between the Mullins-trained **Hurricane Fly**, so impressive during the course of his novice campaign, and this year's Cheltenham-third **Binocular**. The latter appeals as the more solid of the two options. He left an indelible impression when putting Celestial Halo to the sword at Ascot last December and has plausible excuses for failing to uphold that form and justify strong favouritism when they met again at Prestbury Park three months later. Whilst it's true that Binocular raced only three times in 2008/9, the weather played some part in that, and he can be expected to be seen a bit more this time around.

YOUR COPY OF RACING HISTORY

Chapter and verse on 10,000 horses that ran over the jumps in another vintage season

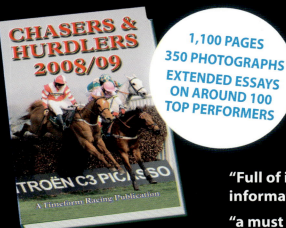

1,100 PAGES
350 PHOTOGRAPHS
EXTENDED ESSAYS ON AROUND 100 TOP PERFORMERS

"Full of indispensable information"

"a must for anyone serious about Jumps racing"

Unbeatable value at £70

CHASE THE STARS

The new Chasers & Hurdlers annual is packed with winning pointers

"Still has the potential to dominate the current two-mile hurdling division and looks very good value for the Champion Hurdle…"

"Looks well equipped to enjoy considerably more success over fences… the Grand Sefton at Aintree is a likely opportunity for him in the autumn."

"Very much a chaser on looks…seems sure to take high rank among the novices in 2009/10."

Find out who in Chasers & Hurdlers 2008/09

CALL OR ORDER ONLINE
01422 330540
timeform.com/shop

THE HOME OF WINNERS SINCE 1948

Ante-Post Betting

There aren't many of the top prizes which have eluded the grasp of Paul Nicholls, but the Grand National remains a notable exception. The Ditcheat handler has been responsible for leading fancies such as Double Thriller, Ad Hoc and My Will, and even offloaded subsequent winner Silver Birch, but he's yet to improve on Royal Auclair's second in 2005. However, he starts out 2009/10 with a strong-looking squad of potential runners. Whether or not Denman competes in the great race remains to be seen, and he'd certainly be some sight attacking the National fences, though if he did he would also serve to compress the weights for a couple of stablemates who may be equally suited by the demands of the race. For all he won a point in Ireland in May 2008, **Tricky Trickster**'s career under Rules was less than five months old when he won the National Hunt Chase at Cheltenham in fine style on what was just his fourth start over fences. That's some testament to his potential, and having been bought out of Nigel Twiston-Davis' yard, we expect him to carry on an upward curve for his new handler. Nicholls is likely to campaign Tricky Trickster over hurdles initially, though he has the National written all over him, and granted a clear run at training it seems inconceivable that he'll be as big as 25/1 on the day.

Another Ditcheat inmate who looks set to prove a regular in the National in years to come is **Big Fella Thanks**. The only novice to take part in the 2009 renewal, he made a really good fist of things in finishing sixth to Mon Mome. The winner of the Skybet at Doncaster before managing an excellent third in the Racing Post Chase, Big Fella Thanks deserves plenty of credit for his Aintree run given his relative lack of experience, keeping on well after a couple of late mistakes had placed him on the back foot as the race was taking shape. He's by no means fully exposed and odds of 33/1 make some appeal at this stage.

Hurricane Fly is a clear favourite for the Champion Hurdle at Cheltenham in March. Whilst that much is understandable given the style with which the Willie Mullins-trained five-year-old has gone about things in his career to date, it's equally true that he's yet to be tested in Britain or outside novice company. His demolition job of Go Native at Leopardstown last December was made to look all the better when that one won the Supreme Novices' in Hurricane Fly's injury-enforced absence, and he supplemented that success with an equally smooth win at the Punchestown Festival, but whether he can prove himself

Binocular's facile win over Celestial Halo (left) suggests he's well worth another try in the Champion Hurdle

against more established two-mile hurdlers remains to be seen. Despite failing to justify short-priced favouritism in the 2009 running of the Champion, **Binocular** still appeals as having leading claims looking towards 2010. The leading juvenile in 2007/8, Binocular really announced his arrival at the top table with a thumping of Celestial Halo in the Grade 2 International Hurdle at Ascot in December. Reportedly held up by the weather thereafter, he didn't go with quite the same zip at Cheltenham three months later when third to stable-companion Punjabi—with his Ascot rival splitting the pair—but that effort removed any lingering doubts regarding his stamina, and it's most likely that McCoy won't be at pains to delay his challenge so much next time. All in all, his prospects look just as good, if not better, for the race this season, certainly making a far more attractive proposition than the pair that edged him out last March, and the odds of 6/1 that are available look very tasty indeed.

Whilst also holding a very strong hand for the Grand National, it will probably come as no surprise to anyone that Paul Nicholls likewise trains the biggest threat to his own Kauto Star as he bids for a third Gold Cup. Having managed a 1-2-3 and a 1-2-4-5 in the last two runnings, stating that he houses the best staying chasers around requires no insight. However, in terms of pure ability it

Will the World Hurdle again be the Cheltenham Festival target for Big Buck's?

may not be Denman or Neptune Collonges who give the reigning champ most to fear, but rather **Big Buck's**. After unseating at the last when still in contention in the Hennessy last November, Big Buck's proved a revelation as a staying hurdler, winning four from four, including the World Hurdle at Cheltenham. It's true that he'd most likely carry all before him if kept to that sphere, but it's also the case that connections may feel there is an element of unfinished business with regards to his chasing career, and if the flaws in his jumping technique can be ironed out we are of the view that he could be the one to give Kauto Star most to think about. With the potential lure of replicating Michael Dickinson's 'Famous Five' in the Gold Cup, it may be that Big Buck's will be called up to swell the ranks. Either way, odds of 20/1 will look huge were he to turn up.

ALL THE EVIDENCE YOU NEED

Over £3000 profit in the first year*

JURY

The tipping service that draws on the expertise of our whole editorial team.

Jury Daily
'Give the Jury a trial'
5 Days £35
10 Days £60

Find out more at **timeform.com/jury**
and join at **timeform.com/shop**

Based on £20 per point at advised prices, 10 Sep 08–09 Sep 09.

THE HOME OF WINNERS SINCE 1948

In Perspective

The daily reports of Timeform's representatives on the course form the basis of *Timeform Perspective*. Their observations, supplemented by those of Timeform's handicappers and comment writers, make *Timeform Perspective* thoroughly informative. Here are some key races from last spring's major Festival meetings in Britain chosen from the Timeform Form-Book.

CHELTENHAM Tuesday, Mar 10

3930 williamhill.com Supreme Nov Hdle (Gr 1) (1) 2m110y (8)
(4yo+) £68,412

3622*	GO NATIVE (IRE) *NMeade,Ireland* 6-11-7 PCarberry 11 12/1	1
2741*	MEDERMIT (FR) *AKing* 5-11-7 RobertThornton 12/1	nk 2
3125³	SOMERSBY (IRE) *MissHCKnight* 5-11-7 DominicElsworth 40/1	2¾ 3
3309²	Copper Bleu (IRE) *PJHobbs* 7-11-7 RichardJohnson 16 14/1	hd 4
3481 ur	Cousin Vinny (IRE) *WPMullins,Ireland* 6-11-7 MrPWMullins 11/4 9/4f	1½ 5
3560*	Red Moloney (USA) *JHowardJohnson* 5-11-7 DenisO'Regan... 12 11/1	hd 6
3384	Shoreacres (IRE) *BGPowell* 6-11-7 WilsonRenwick 25/1	7 7
3588²	Ainama (IRE) *NJHenderson* 5-11-7 APMcCoy 12 14/1	3 8
3426*	Torphichen *DEPipe* 4-10-13 AJMcNamara 11/2 7/1	1 9
2814*	Micheal Flips (IRE) *AndrewTurnell* 5-11-7 MarkGrant 12 9/1	1¼ 10
2741⁴	Golan Way *MissSWest* 5-11-7 JamieGoldstein........................... 28/1	6 11
3223*	Kempes (IRE) *WPMullins,Ireland* 6-11-7 RWalsh......................... 9/1	4 12
3465*	Shamari (FR) *PFNicholls* 5-11-7 ChristianWilliams....................... 66/1	2¾ 13
2143⁵	Leo's Lucky Star (USA) *DEPipe* 7-11-7 (t) TomScudamore....... 50/1	6 14
3125²	Kangaroo Court (IRE) *MissELLavelle* 5-11-7 JackDoyle.............. 25/1	4 15
3706*	Gloucester *MJScudamore* 6-11-7 JohnKington 150/1	16 16
3829	Bee Sting *MrsLWilliamson* 5-11-7 DerekLaverty....................... 250/1	22 17
3637	Intensifier (IRE) *DLWilliams* 5-11-7 SEDurack........................... 200/1	29 18
3588⁶	Alarazi (IRE) *TGMills* 5-11-7 JamieMoore................................. 100/1	pu
2756 ur	Leamington Lad (IRE) *NATwiston-Davies* 6-11-7 (b) PJBrennan ... 100/1	pu

1.30race Docado Syndicate 20ran 4m01.09

No more than an average renewal of the Supreme Novices', only Cousin Vinny arguably having shown form good enough to win any of the last 5 runnings and only 3 of the field having won even at Grade 2 level, though the trio included the first 2 home; less than 5 lengths covered the first 6 home, though the first 2, for differing reasons, could have finished a little further clear than they did, while unusually for this race prospective chasers had the upper hand over the smart Flat recruits, only one of the first 7 seeming sure to be just a hurdler; the pace was fair at best, with the leader largely ignored, and plenty were taking a good hold early, the time very similar to that for the Champion Hurdle, though that was run at a much quicker tempo and a shower of rain in between negates time comparisons. **Go Native** looked as well as any beforehand and showed smart form in gaining a fourth win in 6 starts over hurdles, travelling well waited with, not fluent on occasions but getting a good run on the inside to lead before the last, quickening clear then idling markedly and only just holding on; his turn of foot was the decisive factor, as it had been last time, and it would be no surprise if he didn't stay so well as his pedigree suggests; he was quoted afterwards for the 2010 Champion Hurdle, though the horse that probably ought to have been quoted was the absent Hurricane Fly who beat him so comprehensively at Leopardstown, he himself seeming more an Arkle candidate. **Medermit**, who looked very well, was unlucky, going well when stumbling before 3 out and then hampered at the last when beginning to run on well, still finishing strongly; he's done well over hurdles, and although not a traditional chasing type in the style of the third and fourth he is athletic and likely to make a chaser when the time comes. **Somersby**, on his toes and looking in good shape, was the most imposing of these and ran a race full of promise, coming from further off the pace than the first 2, going well held up until making a mistake 3 out, shaken up after and staying on well once finding his stride in the straight, nearest at the finish; he should make a smashing chaser next season. **Copper Bleu**, who looked very well, has progressed with each run over hurdles and showed form nearing smart here, travelling strongly for a long way, disputing the lead into the straight but unable to quicken under pressure, losing third near the line; he ran well in a good renewal of the Aintree bumper last spring and may well get another chance at this sort of level there next month, when he might be worth stepping back up in trip, though he's not short of speed. **Cousin Vinny**, reportedly not at his best after arriving from Ireland, didn't take the eye particularly beforehand and ran below expectations, well placed 2 out after being waited with but ridden and unable to quicken into the straight, hanging left and, as in all his previous races over hurdles, making a mistake at the last, no extra after; he's not really developed physically since last season, still rather unfurnished, and on balance his form over hurdles doesn't quite match the expectations held of him on his bumper form; he will, though, almost certainly benefit from being stepped up to 2½m and would surely have been better off in the Baring Bingham here, and might well have run in that but for the absence of Hurricane Fly. **Red Moloney** was just about the best of these on the Flat and, having been odds on for his 3 wins at Musselburgh, he ran well in this much stronger grade, tracking the leaders going well, making a mistake 3 out and ridden and one paced in the straight; he was a weak finisher on the Flat and not to be trusted but he's not done anything much wrong so far over hurdles, though he lacks the physique to think there's a lot more to come from him. **Shoreacres** ran creditably, having the run of things to a large extent, racing second to halfway, remaining close up but ridden 3 out and one paced at the next, looking ready for a step back up in trip, his dam Call Me Dara having been a staying chaser (won the Paddy Power at Leopardstown); he too is likely to make a chaser. **Ainama** looked very well but he was a bit below form, sent for home earlier than previously, leading after the fourth but headed 2 out and unable to quicken, his jumping again not the most fluent, with mistakes at the fifth and last noted; he may do better faced with more of a test of stamina, provided his jumping doesn't hold him back, while it would be no surprise, given his Flat record, to see him aimed in the meantime at the Chester Cup. **Torphichen** failed to build on his 2 wins in this much stronger race, running here in preference to the Triumph but shaping as if more of a test of stamina in that might have suited him better, well placed the way the race went, but tapped for foot as the tempo picked up 2 out; he's still relatively inexperienced, this just his seventh race of any kind, so there may yet be more to come. **Micheal Flips**, on softer ground than previously, was below form in this better company, making an effort after 3 out having been held up but little impression; he'd looked promising previously and is the type that could do even better as a chaser next season. **Golan Way** made the running as usual and had a soft lead, largely ignored by the rest, but he soon lost his place after a bad mistake at the fourth and weakened 3 out, running well below form. **Kempes**' record suggested he could progress and make an impact at this level but a blunder at the first didn't help and he never really threatened, beaten by 3 out. **Shamari** needed to improve markedly to figure, back up in class, and having not jumped well he was struggling by the fifth. **Leo's**

Lucky Star was a fair way below form on his first start since November, always towards the rear. **Kangaroo Court** looked very well and, along with the third, was about the nicest type in the field but he wasn't able to show to advantage, perhaps lack of experience combined with lack of speed his undoing, for he couldn't pick up when ridden 3 out and finished well held; he's the type to make a chaser next season. **Gloucester** faced a stiff task in this company, and having been held up as usual he was always in rear and made a mistake at the fourth. **Intensifier**, yet to win a race, was well out of his depth. **Alarazi** was again highly tried and nowhere near up to the task at this stage. **Leamington Lad** faced a stiff task in this company on his first start in nearly 3 months and made no show.

3931	Irish Independent Arkle Challenge Trophy Chase (Gr 1) (1) (5yo+) £96,917		2m (12)	
3482 [2]	FORPADYDEPLASTERER (IRE) *ThomasCooper,Ireland* 7-11-7 BJGeraghty		8/1	1
3337 *	KALAHARI KING (FR) *FerdyMurphy* 8-11-7 GLee		11 8/1	sh 2
3079 *	PLANET OF SOUND *PJHobbs* 7-11-7 RichardJohnson		10/1	5 3
3500 *	Made In Taipan (IRE) *ThomasMullins,Ireland* 7-11-7 DNRussell		20/1	3¾ 4
3402 *	Tartak (FR) *TRGeorge* 6-11-7 PJBrennan		11 10/1	1¾ 5
3569 *	Gauvain (GER) *CJMann* 7-11-7 (s) NoelFehily		33/1	ns 6
3569 [2]	Cornas (NZ) *NickWilliams* 7-11-7 DarylJacob		33/1	1 7
3311 *	I'msingingtheblues (IRE) *PFNicholls* 7-11-7 ChristianWilliams		8 9/1	nk 8
3234 [3]	Follow The Plan (IRE) *OliverMcKiernan,Ireland* 6-11-7 JCullen		16/1	2¾ 9
3121 [2]	Calgary Bay (IRE) *MissHCKnight* 6-11-7 APMcCoy		7 15/2	10 10
3569 [4]	Panjo Bere (FR) *GLMoore* 6-11-7 (s) JamieMoore		40/1	9 11
3121 [4]	Cool Operator *JHowardJohnson* 6-11-7 DenisO'Regan		125/1	1 12
3079 [5]	Cheating Chance (IRE) *AndrewTurnell* 8-11-7 MarkGrant		150/1	1 13
3234 *	Golden Silver (FR) *WPMullins,Ireland* 7-11-7 PaulTownend		14/1	4½ 14
3468 *	Bringbackthebiff (NZ) *EJO'Grady,Ireland* 7-11-7 (t) AJMcNamara		33/1	18 15
2864 [2]	Tatenen (FR) *PFNicholls* 5-11-7 RWalsh		4/1f	f
2882 *	Original (FR) *MRolland,France* 7-11-7 JamesDavies		16/1	pu
2.05race Goat Racing Syndicate 17ran 4m00.94				

An open-betting heat and indeed a bunched finish was indicative of a relatively ordinary bunch of 2-mile novices, one lacking a standout performer who might trouble the top 2-milers next season, and, given the way the division has gone so far, there's nothing to suggest this form will stand up in other graded events upcoming; the race was at least a fair test, the first 4 split evenly between prominently-ridden and hold-up horses, Made In Taipan the pacesetter. **Forpadydeplasterer** had been beaten 3 times in graded company since a successful chasing debut, twice around 2½m, and though showing a little improvement here he doesn't really appeal as the type who'll develop into a genuine Championship contender next season, turned out in the peak of condition, and all out after striking for home turning in, proving game as the second came with momentum; there's no doubting he jumps well, but at Punchestown it could just as easily be the runner-up, or even something else, that comes out on top. **Kalahari King** left previous form well behind when fourth in the Supreme Novices' last season and did so again at this meeting after a relatively low-key grounding, establishing himself as a smart chaser, too, in going down only narrowly under an excellent waiting ride, travelling strongly and looking set to sweep right by the winner when produced after the last only for that one to find marginally more in the battle; clearly not himself for his only previous defeat over fences, he'll be a leading contender in the 2m novices at Aintree and Punchestown (won at that meeting over hurdles last season) now, with those tracks likely to play to his strengths even more, and as a notably fluent jumper he looks sure to make up into a good-class 2m handicapper next season. **Planet of Sound** justified his participation at the expense of a handicap campaign, and there's an even smarter performance in him if his jumping comes right, having a tendency to miss the odd one at present, which counted against him in this larger and better-quality field as he was rather on the back foot after the eighth, doing well in the circumstances, another awkward jump at the last no barrier to his seeing the race out. **Made In Taipan** hadn't been seen to best effect behind

Follow The Plan and Tatenen on his first try in a Grade 1 novice, but he had a previous verdict over the winner that day and gave a much truer reflection of himself in getting the better of that horse again, his being able to lead probably playing no small part, travelling and jumping with plenty of fluency, doing enough to suggest he isn't reliant on very testing ground, and a minor error at the last probably prevented him from finishing a length or 2 closer. **Tartak** was a deal more convincing than on his previous visit to Cheltenham, looking accomplished, as he had elsewhere, and, trying the minimum trip for the first time in Britain, would have confirmed himself smart and finished nearer third granted a trouble-free run, ridden more patiently in mid-field and squeezed out both after the eighth and landing over the last, when holding that position, though he made a minor error of his own at that fence; one of the Aintree handicaps could suit him, given his ability to jump at speed. **Gauvain** confirmed Kingmaker superiority over Cornas, though he was arguably fortunate once again, his performance most significant in highlighting his jumping frailties, rarely fluent and trailing for much of the last mile before keeping on through beaten horses; whilst undoubtedly useful, he's unlikely to make much appeal in competitive races until his jumping becomes more assured. **Cornas** looks the ideal type for the Red Rum at Aintree, a strong-travelling sort who's almost certainly better than he's shown so far over fences, unfortunate to be edged out in a Grade 2 last time and going best of all in the firing line here when a stumble on landing 2 out put paid to his chance, not that he'd definitely have won, tiring up the hill; a sound jumper overall, who looked outstanding in condition, he had less chasing experience than any of these after just 2 starts and will be well suited by a sharp 2m. **I'msingingtheblues**' handicap form hasn't been working out especially well, but he'd built up a good record over fences, his only defeat coming at the hands of Briareus, and it's most likely he wasn't at his best here, ridden to have every chance in touch, but at work from 4 out and never any closer than on the heels of the leaders. **Follow The Plan**'s beating of Tatenen might not be worth all it looked, finishing behind fourth-placed Made In Taipan the other 2 times they have met, and, after heavy ground had appeared a possible excuse for a subdued showing at back at Leopardstown, conditions should have been in his favour here, yet he was already struggling to hold his place when a mistake 2 out sealed his fate. **Calgary Bay**'s form failed to stand up at all here, others intertwined struggling, too, though that's not to say he won't still go on and fulfil previous expectations, again jumping well on the whole (not fluent ninth) and travelling easily only to make no further impression after 3 out; concerns over the consistency of his stable are also worth noting, for all he looked outstanding in condition. **Panjo Bere**'s Ascot success is beginning to look flattering, at least in terms of his capabilities at 2m, things rather set up that day, whilst he's got nowhere that form in 2 starts since, tried in cheekpieces here only to be flat out towards the rear fully 4 out; he is likely to prove best back over 2½m. **Cool Operator** is a fairly useful novice but he's been badly exposed in 2 starts in graded company; he's likely to prove best back at 2½m+. **Cheating Chance** looks to have lost his way, not that he had a very realistic chance tried again in graded company; he looked in excellent condition. **Golden Silver**, who'd beaten the winner last time, in another twist to muddling form lines, isn't necessarily a one-dimensional mudlark, showing up well for a long way under a positive ride, though he seemed wanting for speed as he lost his place going to 2 out and may well need further if he's to show anything like his form under these conditions. **Bringbackthebiff** remains unexposed as a chaser having been impressive when winning an 2¼m maiden in heavy going last time, this seemingly too much of a test, probably for speed, possibly ability. **Tatenen**, ante-post favourite since the autumn, was arguably priced more on reputation than the substance of his form but may still justify it, his jumping having looked anything but a concern overall for all he failed to get beyond the third here. **Original**'s size raised concerns over his effectiveness on an undulating track but above all he can't have been right, his being hampered by the faller at the third possibly behind it, soon detached and pulled up shortly after.

3933 Smurfit Kappa Champion Hdle Challenge Trophy (Gr 1) (1) (4yo+) £210,937 — 2m110y (8)

3461[3]	PUNJABI *NJHenderson* 6-11-10 BJGeraghty		22/1		1
3315[*]	CELESTIAL HALO (IRE) *PFNicholls* 5-11-10 (t) RWalsh		17/2	nk	2
2754[*]	BINOCULAR (FR) *NJHenderson* 5-11-10 APMcCoy		6/4f	hd	3
2754[5]	Crack Away Jack *MissECLavelle* 5-11-10 NoelFehily		16/1	2¼	4
3236[2]	Muirhead (IRE) *NMeade,Ireland* 6-11-10 DJCondon		33/1	2¾	5
2754[4]	Katchit (IRE) *AKing* 6-11-10 RobertThornton	14	12/1	nk	6
3126[3]	Snap Tie (IRE) *PJHobbs* 7-11-10 RichardJohnson		40/1	8	7
2207[3]	Jered (IRE) *NMeade,Ireland* 7-11-10 DJCasey		33/1	3¼	8
3236[5]	Hardy Eustace (IRE) *DTHughes,Ireland* 12-11-10 (v+t) PWFlood		100/1	½	9
2952[2]	Won In The Dark (IRE) *SabrinaJoanHarty,Ireland* 5-11-10 DNRussell		33/1	3	10
3315[2]	Osana (FR) *DEPipe* 7-11-10 (b) AJMcNamara	10	13/2	¾	11
3461[2]	Whiteoak (IRE) *DMcCainJnr* 6-11-3 JasonMaguire		16/1	3¼	12
2816[3]	Blue Bajan (IRE) *AndrewTurnell* 7-11-10 GLee		80/1	3¼	13
2756[*]	Sentry Duty (FR) *NJHenderson* 7-11-10 AndrewTinkler		33/1	5	14
3236[4]	Sublimity (FR) *RobertAlanHennessy,Ireland* 9-11-10 (t) PACarberry		20/1	14	15
3315[4]	Alph *RATeal* 12-11-10 ColinBolger		250/1	7	16
2816[*]	Harchibald (FR) *NMeade,Ireland* 10-11-10 (t) PCarberry		33/1	¾	17
3236[*]	Brave Inca (IRE) *ColmAMurphy,Ireland* 11-11-10 DominicElsworth		25/1	3¼	18
3461[*]	Ashkazar (FR) *DEPipe* 5-11-10 (b) TimmyMurphy	16	14/1	2½	19
3775[*]	Ebaziyan (IRE) *WPMullins,Ireland* 8-11-10 PaulTownend		50/1	2¾	20
3236[3]	River Liane (FR) *ThomasCooper,Ireland* 5-11-10 NPMadden		125/1	10	21
755[5]	Othermix (FR) *TRGeorge* 5-11-10 PJBrennan		100/1		f
	Cybergenic (FR) *PaulMurphy* 11-11-10 KeithMercer		250/1		pu

3.20race Mr Raymond Tooth 23ran 4m00.87

Whilst the ante-post market had long had a one-sided look to it this proved anything but the crowning of Binocular, who was instead upstaged by his stablemate in an gripping 3-way finish, the winner returning a figure a little below what the favourite had achieved in his prep; a similar time to the Supreme earlier on the card was by no means indicative of a similar gallop, a shower between the 2 having had an effect, this run at genuine Championship pace after a couple had gone up to contest Osana's lead at the third, the field soon strung out, with Crack Away Jack doing best of those held up. **Punjabi** has come far since fourth in the Triumph 2 years back and advanced again from his third to Katchit on his first attempt at this race, looking a different horse to in his prep at Wincanton, blooming in condition, and showing there's more to him as a hurdler than just speed, keeping the leaders in his sights and determinedly grinding the second down when Geraghty finally went for everything after the last; he's arguably unlucky not to have become the first winner of WBX's £1m bonus, winning 2 of the 3 legs and falling when holding every chance in the other, but there's still the Punchestown Champion to boost the coffers, which he won last year (also won Grade 1 juvenile at meeting). **Celestial Halo** couldn't have gone much closer to emulating Katchit and following up Triumph success in the Champion, this course again bringing out the best in him, arguably deserving extra credit having helped force the pace as the pair he split sat slightly off it, digging in gamely, though Binocular does still have a 2-1 verdict over him, much more decisive in his 2 wins, too; Celestial Halo remains likely to be suited by further than 2m and, whilst his trainer suggested he may not be seen again this season having been beaten at Liverpool last year, the Aintree Hurdle could be the ideal opportunity for a step up, particularly with Punabi and Binocular looking specialist 2-milers; further down the line, it was reported he may have chasing put on hold for another crack at this race next year. **Binocular** remains the highest rated hurdler in training, one likely to win a Champion Hurdle in years to come, here rubbishing concerns over his stamina on this course for all he was beaten at Cheltenham for the second successive year (runner-up in Supreme), still closing steadily at the finish, lacking his usual zip if anything, reportedly held up by the weather after Ascot; he's unlikely to run again this season according to his trainer. **Crack Away Jack** delivered the performance he'd long promised, not quite up to bustling up the front 3 but proving himself high-class nevertheless, ridden as he'd been in the Fred Winter last year, creeping closer from well back going down the hill (travelled powerfully), briefly looking like coming right through again before flattening out; he already looks a leading contender for next year's Arkle, built for chasing, whilst there will be few novice chasers with hurdles form comparable to his. **Muirhead**, who'd been co-favourite alongside Binocular when down the field in the Supreme last year, gave a truer reflection of his ability this time, confirming himself a very smart hurdler, running to a similar level to when chasing home Brave Inca in the Irish version, holding a similar position throughout, very soft ground evidently not essential provided he's given a test. **Katchit** was better for being freshened up, though this was a stronger renewal than the one he'd won last year whilst he seemed to find the less testing ground against him, too, shaping as though he'll be suited by further these days ideally, running through rivals only late as he typically dug in; now looking worth a try in headgear (connections have considered such a move already), it's possible he'll work towards the World Hurdle in 2009/10 given his diminutive build rather rules out chasing. **Snap Tie**'s defeat of Katchit in October had rather been devalued by subsequent events, and, whilst he'd gone close in the Christmas Hurdle, he fared about as well as could be expected in this company, putting a poor showing behind him for all he could never get fully competitive from rear, short of room briefly turning in. **Jered**, who'd been amongst the market leaders for this in the autumn, has rather come up short on his last 2 starts, having conditions as a potential excuse last time, but essentially failing to measure up in the jumping department faced with a very different test to previously here, sluggish and in rear for the majority of the race and flattered by his finishing position having bounded past tiring rivals late. **Hardy Eustace**, the Champion of 2004 and 2005, has succumbed to age in recent seasons but ran his heart out as ever, helping force the gallop and fading only on the run to 2 out. **Won In The Dark** has built on his Triumph third to Celestial Halo in Ireland this season but this race didn't play to his strengths as the Festival Hurdle had, and, after making a brief effort coming down the hill, he was held by 2 out. **Osana**, runner-up to Katchit last year, is lightly raced overall but his campaigning this season suggests he's had problems and, surprisingly tried blinkered, he went backwards from his return 5 weeks earlier, forcing the gallop initially but struggling from the top of the hill. **Whiteoak**'s defence of her David Nicholson crown was passed over for this bigger prize, but she might well have also struggled in that lesser event, the winner there raising the bar, whilst she wasn't near her best, anyway, having failed to jump with any real fluency in rear; this possibly came too soon after Wincanton. **Blue Bajan** was in no position to make the most of the end-to-end gallop after mistakes at 2 of the first 3 flights. **Sentry Duty** has been campaigned sparingly with his trainer of the opinion that he's best fresh, but he ran no sort of race in the Supreme last year and followed suit upped in grade again here, getting off on the wrong foot with a mistake at the first and never dangerous. **Sublimity**, first and fourth in the last 2 renewals, had scoped badly on his most recent start and possibly had something amiss again, sweating up beforehand and running poorly, making only a brief effort coming down the hill. **Alph** was out of his depth though ran poorly nonetheless, struggling as early as the fifth. **Harchibald** had his day in the Christmas Hurdle, and, whilst looking a picture beforehand, was in nothing like the same form 2½ months on, trailing throughout. **Brave Inca** has done much at this meeting over the years, Champion in 2006, but, whilst he'd won the Irish version in the mud in January, he looked a shadow of his former self under these conditions, losing his place after the fourth. **Ashkazar** has shown his form only once from 3 starts this season, when having a below-par Punjabi behind, losing his place from the fifth here tried blinkered. **Ebaziyan**'s Supreme success in 2007 seems a long time ago now. **River Liane** has bombed out on both starts at the Festival, second favourite for the Fred Winter last year (bled). **Othermix**, a Grade 2 winner at Auteuil, had finished fifth in a Grade 1 there on his final start for Arnaud Chaille-Chaille (Hurricane Fly and Quevega placed) but made little impact set a stiff task for his British debut, midfield and beaten when departing 3 out; a Linamix half-brother to Oh Crick, he has the size to make a chaser himself.

CHELTENHAM Wednesday, Mar 11

3944 Ballymore Nov Hdle (Baring Bingham) (Gr 1) 2m5f (10)
(1) (4yo+) £68,412

3349*	MIKAEL D'HAGUENET (FR) *WPMullins,Ireland* 5-11-7 RWalsh	11/4 5/2f	1
3125*	KARABAK (FR) *AKing* 6-11-7 APMcCoy	10/3 4/1	1¾ 2
3201*	DIAMOND HARRY *NickWilliams* 6-11-7 TimmyMurphy	9/2 4/1	3¾ 3
3025*	China Rock (IRE) *MFMorris,Ireland* 6-11-7 NPMadden	25/1	nk 4
3730*	Knockara Beau (IRE) *GACharlton* 5-11-7 JanFaltejsek	16 14/1	3¾ 5
2406*	The Nightingale (FR) *PFNicholls* 6-11-7 ChristianWilliams	12 14/1	10 6
3533*	Realt Dubh (IRE) *NMeade,Ireland* 5-11-7 PCarberry	20/1	6 7
3080*	Mad Max (IRE) *NJHenderson* 7-11-7 BJGeraghty	6/1	1½ 8
3409²	Ruthenoise (FR) *DEPipe* 4-10-5 TomScudamore	100/1	10 9
3212²	Junior *AKing* 6-11-7 (b) RobertThornton	33 16/1	23 10
3624	Dorset Square (IRE) *JohnJosephMurphy,Ireland* 5-11-7 AJMcNamara	200/1	dist 11
3542*	Quwetwo *JHowardJohnson* 6-11-7 DenisO'Regan	20/1	7 12
2773*	Quartetto (GER) *MervynTorrens,Ireland* 5-11-7 APThornton	100/1	29 13
3755⁵	Richard The Third *JohnAHarris* 5-11-7 SEDurack	250/1	pu

2.05race Mrs S. Ricci 14ran 5m16.56

A very strong renewal of this long-standing Grade 1, which has arguably lost some of its lustre since the introduction of the Spa Hurdle in 2005; the winner had carried all before him in Ireland this winter and beat a couple with similar profiles in Britain, whilst the bare form shouldn't be used to devalue their potential, as a steady gallop (things didn't pick up until 3 out) dictated that they were unable to achieve quite what they might have done. **Mikael d'Haguenet** extended his unbeaten run for this stable to 5 and is clearly more than just a mudlark, every bit as impressive on this bigger stage, looking one who's capable of producing more still at Punchestown and Auteuil before he's put away for another stab at chasing next season—whichever route connections choose, it almost goes without saying that he remains very much one to follow; whilst he'll stay further, he again impressed with his speed, having no problem quickening as the gallop did and soon through a narrow gap to take control after 2 out, doing no more than required in front. **Karabak** is a hurdler in appearance, having nothing like the presence of the chasing prospects he split here, but there's better to come from him nevertheless, his Ascot success (changed hands since) advertised by Somersby in the previous day's Supreme, whilst this falsely-run race didn't play to his strengths, not fluent 3 times as the gallop was increasing and shuffled back as a result, then forced to come wide as he challenged in the straight; he could well develop into a leading staying hurdler in 2009/10 should connections keep him to the smaller obstacles. **Diamond Harry**, deposed as favourite since the 6-day stage having held that position for much of the season, produced another smart performance for all he met with his first defeat, having his chance as he got to the front going okay 2 out, looking ungainly though as he struggled to match the winner's turn of speed and all out to hold third in the end after a mistake at the last; he's likely to be put away for chasing next season. **China Rock** has progressed into a very useful novice, this another major step forward from his Cork win at 2¼m, looking value for the improvement too for all that this race possibly isn't the most reliable form overall; bred more for this longer trip, he maintained his position in comparison to the markets leaders as others dropped away, almost getting up for third in the end. **Knockara Beau** underlined his recent improvement, albeit rather having his limitations exposed at the same time, moving up into the firing line by 2 out only to be outclassed in the straight, seeing the race out for all that the principals got away; rather like several of these, he has the potential to make at least as good a novice chaser next season. **The Nightingale**'s previous hurdles runs have stood up well, and, whilst he came up short faced with this first major test, there's still time for him to fulfil his potential, returning from 3 months off here, whilst matters weren't truly run either—The Nightingale was one of the first at work 4 out and struggling badly after the next. **Realt Dubh** is a useful novice but he's been put in his place each time he's been asked to tackle top company, upped in trip here, which his pedigree gave hope he'd stay, only to be left behind from 3 out. **Mad Max**'s breathing had been operated on since Newbury but, despite looking in excellent condition, he left the impression all wasn't right as he met with his first defeat, going out tamely after a mistake 2 from home (not unduly knocked about), with the longer trip unlikely to have been an issue given how the race had been run (bred to stay too), acknowledging he'd taken a while to settle; he remains the type to make at least as good a chaser. **Ruthenoise** will appeal back in ordinary novice company under a penalty but faced an unrealistic task here, whilst her stamina at the trip shouldn't be judged on this either, weakening after 3 out. **Junior** has long been exposed, looking held by Diamond Harry on Newbury running, but that proved irrelevant as he took little interest anyway, his attitude seemingly becoming a bigger and bigger problem. **Dorset Square** is fully exposed as being little better than modest, having zero chance in this grade. **Quwetwo** had his limitations exposed as a hurdler, his shortcomings rooted in his jumping and he soon dropped out from the top of the hill. **Quartetto** failed to make the grade in top bumpers and it was a similar story with this step-up in class over hurdles, though there's mileage in him yet in this sphere with his sights lowered; his jumping still needs work and it let him down badly in the face of an unrealistic task here. **Richard The Third** was totally outclassed.

3945	RSA Chase (Gr 1) (1) (5yo+) £96,917	3m110y (19)
3482°	COOLDINE (IRE) *WPMullins,Ireland* 7-11-4 RWalsh 3 9/4f	1
3346°	HORNER WOODS (IRE) *MrsJHarrington,Ireland* 7-11-4 RMPower	16 2
		66/1
3316²	MASSINI'S MAGUIRE (IRE) *PJHobbs,* 8-11-4 RichardJohnson 10/1	9 3
3439°	Carruthers *MBradstock* 6-11-4 MattieBatchelor 7 13/2	4 4
2923°	Casey Jones (IRE) *NMeade,Ireland* 8-11-4 (t) PCarberry 12 16/1	1 5
2628°	What A Friend *PFNicholls* 6-11-4 SamThomas 11/2 13/2	nk 6
3503°	Siegemaster (IRE) *DTHughes,Ireland* 8-11-4 (s) DNRussell....... 20 16/1	f
3299⁴	Bohemian Lass (IRE) *WHarney,Ireland* 6-10-11 JCullen............. 150/1	f
3439²	Ballyfitz *NATwiston-Davies* 9-11-4 PJBrennan............................ 16/1	pu
2944°	Gone To Lunch (IRE) *JScott* 9-11-4 (s) APMcCoy........................ 8 7/1	pu
3743¹	Hold Em (IRE) *WKGoldsworthy* 7-11-4 GLee 66/1	pu
3228°	Killyglen (IRE) *JHowardJohnson* 7-11-4 DenisO'Regan............... 12/1	pu
3650⁴	Lightning Strike (GER) *MissVenetiaWilliams* 6-11-4 AColeman ... 28/1	pu
3242 pu	Lodge Lane (IRE) *VRADartnall* 8-11-4 ChristianWilliams 33/1	pu
2815⁴	The Market Man (NZ) *NJHenderson* 9-11-4 BJGeraghty............. 14/1	pu
2.40race Mrs V. O'Leary 15ran 6m22.99		

A good renewal of the premier prize for staying novice chasers, one run at a strong pace, and while those who helped force that gallop perhaps did themselves no favours, the winner was most impressive and showed form up there with good recent winners of this race, including subsequent Gold Cup winners Looks Like Trouble and Denman. **Cooldine**, who looked very well, produced a performance on a par with that posted by Looks Like Trouble in 1999 and Denman in 2007 (both subsequent Gold Cup winners) and he's clearly a top-notch novice, who'll be a serious challenger to the very best staying chasers in 2009/10; Cooldine impressed with both his jumping (slight mistake fifteenth) and the way he travelled in this strongly-run race, whilst the amount he found when shaken up (led on bridle 2 out) illustrates that he clearly stays this sort of trip very well; he has a slightly awkward head carriage under pressure but that is nothing to worry about and he's clearly a worthy successor to his connections' mulitple Grade 1-winning chaser Florida Pearl (winner of this race back in 1998). **Horner Woods**, faced with a totally different test, ran well above his previous level of form (including hurdles) but he looks the part and deserves to be credited with that improvement, impressing with the way he travelled despite a few minor mistakes, making headway 3 out and chasing the winner after the next but making no impression, still coming clear of those more involved in forcing the pace; he will stay beyond 3m and is likely to win more races. **Massini's Maguire** was perhaps ridden a little more prominently than ideal given how things unfolded and paid for it in the end, running below form, but he acquitted himself well in the main, ridden after 4 out and sticking to his task well enough to regain a place after the last, his jumping holding up better than might have been expected; he's only had 4 runs over fences so may yet do better in this sphere, with valuable staying handicaps appealing as his targets for 2009/10. **Carruthers** surely couldn't win with the tactics applied and he ran a lot better than the distances indicate (shaped like second best horse on the day), setting a strong pace, largely jumping well but ridden when blundering badly 3 out and having nothing left when headed at the next; he's taken well to fences and hopefully this hard race won't leave a mark, as he should make an impact in good staying handicaps next season. **Casey Jones**, who looked very well, was below form but ran an odd race, held up and making a mistake at the fifteenth, looking quickly beaten approaching 3 out (rider seemed to accept matters) before running on after the last, going on at the finish; he's better than the bare result and might be worth trying in headgear. **What A Friend** was in a more demanding race than previously over fences and, though the run of it ought to have suited the patient tactics employed, he seemed let down by his attitude more than anything else, not really applying himself when asked for his effort on the final circuit and never looking likely to get on terms after a mistake 4 out when fourth and ridden; he's got the ability to win further races over fences, but he's plenty to prove at this level. **Siegemaster** was tried in cheekpieces but his jumping again proved a problem over these more demanding fences and he fell at the eighth when tracking the pace. **Bohemian Lass** fell at the third. **Ballyfitz** found this much too demanding and, as at Ascot last time, turned in a laboured effort, not fluent at times and in rear until pulled up 4 out. **Gone To Lunch**, tried in cheekpieces, made a very bad mistake at the ninth and that seemed to unsettle him (lost place completely), for he took little interest after, dropping out on the final circuit and behind when pulled up 4 out. **Hold Em** possibly hadn't got over his fall last time and was behind until pulled up at the fourteenth, having hit the tenth. **Killyglen** found this a step too far at this stage of his career, his jumping not standing up to the demands of it, though he travelled well for a long way and was still just about in touch when a bad mistake at the fifteenth ended his chance; he may yet make a smart chaser. **Lightning Strike** faced a stiffish task and, although he was up with the pace for a circuit, he hit the tenth and gradually weakened, well tailed off when pulled up on the run-in. **Lodge Lane** hadn't jumped well or applied himself when well held in the Spa Hurdle last season and it was the same story here, always in rear, not fluent at times and labouring badly by the eleventh (also gave trouble in preliminaries). **The Market Man** was sweating beforehand and ran as if all wasn't well, taken wide, failing to settle and dropping out tamely 5 out, pulled up 3 out.

3946 Seasons Holidays Queen Mother Champion Chase   2m (12)
(Gr 1) (1) (5yo+) £182,432

3122²	MASTER MINDED (FR) *PFNicholls* 6-11-10 RWalsh 1/3 4/11f		1
	WELL CHIEF (GER) *PFPipe* 10-11-10 TimmyMurphy 12/1		7 2
3122²	PETIT ROBIN (FR) *NJHenderson* 6-11-10 BJGeraghty 12/1		2 3
3469⁴	Newmill (IRE) *JohnJosephMurphy,Ireland* 11-11-10 RMPower ... 100/1		1½ 4
3351³	Scotsirish (IRE) *WPMullins,Ireland* 8-11-10 PaulTownend 40/1		5 5
3122³	Mahogany Blaze (FR) *NATwiston-Davies* 7-11-10 PJBrennan 40/1		7 6
3461⁵	Ashley Brook (IRE) *KBishop* 11-11-10 RichardJohnson 66/1		11 7
2892*	Santa's Son (IRE) *JHowardJohnson* 9-11-10 (t) DenisO'Regan 33/1		15 8
3456³	Marodima (FR) *MissRebeccaCurtis* 6-11-10 NickScholfield 100/1		dist 9
3351¹	Big Zeb (IRE) *ColmAMurphy,Ireland* 8-11-10 RobertThornton ... 12/1		f
2817⁴	Briareus *AMBalding* 9-11-10 APMcCoy 16/1		f
2885⁶	Twist Magic (FR) *PFNicholls* 7-11-10 (t) SamThomas 20 16/1		f

3.20race Mr Clive D. Smith 12ran 3m59.41

A race that further marked the dominance of Master Minded, who produced yet another top-class performance for all he wasn't so impressive as he'd been 12 months previously; Marodima went with typical zest in front (caused 2 falses starts) and most of those behind the winner made at least one mistake jumping at pace. **Master Minded** became the first horse since Viking Flagship in 1994/5 to land back-to-back Champion Chases and could potentially dominate the division for seasons to come (odds as short as 4/1 offered for him to win the next 2 renewals too), none of those that ran in the previous day's Arkle looking much of a threat, and he has age on his side as a 6-y-o too; it's hard to find a weakness in him, unbeaten in his last 6 starts at 2m and most assured with his jumping now, winning this by daylight despite not seeming in the same imperious form he'd been either last year or earlier this term, joining issue going easily at the ninth and soon in control when shaken up turning in for all he could do no more than maintain his advantage up the hill; it appears Aintree is off the agenda for the time being and, if he is to run again this year, Punchestown is likely to be the venue. **Well Chief**, one of a trio of outstanding 2-milers alongside Moscow Flyer and Azertyuiop in 2004/5, evidently retains his enthusiasm and a high-class level of ability for all injury has limited him to just 4 appearances since then (missed 2008/9 due to heat in a leg), looking the chief threat to Master Minded's crown near to hand if he can be kept sound, likely to have finished a more clear-cut second here but for shortening into 3 out as the pair he split were winding things up in front, getting going to take that position after the last; he failed to stay in the Melling Chase 2 years back, but may yet avoid the winner if sticking to 2m for the Celebration Chase at Sandown (a race he won in 2005). **Petit Robin** came of age to a point as he belatedly produced the very smart performance his Newbury handicap success had promised, his trainer of the opinion the return to a left-handed track played a part; it's hard to see how he'll make much more of an impact on the first 2, however, recovering from a mistake at the fifth and taking the fight to Master Minded as he quickened on before 3 out, unable to get that one off the bridle though and brushed aside turning in, another error at the last inconsequential to his being run out of second. **Newmill**, the Champion of 2006, ran just about his best race since then, though it may not pay to expect him to build on this, never threatening to get amongst the first 3 under a patient ride (bad mistake first), merely running on late. **Scotsirish** has established himself as a smart chaser in recent months but remains some way short of the best, never able to go with the front 3, eventually run out of fourth after the last (his being hampered there making little difference). **Mahogany Blaze** had been put firmly in his place by Master Minded at Ascot but might have done a bit better here with a clear run, held up and badly hampered 4 out as he was beginning to take closer order. **Ashley Brook**, in the thick of things when departing at the last 2 years ago, continues to prove best ignored at this sort of level nowadays. **Santa's Son** failed to take the eye beforehand and ran poorly regardless of the severity of his task; there should still be mileage in him back in handicaps, however, given his rate of improvement since joining this stable. **Marodima**'s Uttoxeter improvement isn't necessarily solid but this was a very stiff task even if it is to be believed and his contribution was to ensure a good pace, charging the tape twice before the starter finally let them go, and he was a spent force by 4 out. **Big Zeb** was robbed of his chance to measure up against the best in Britain, crashing out in a heavy fall 4 out when beginning to take closer order; he remains the highest-rated Irish 2-miler, reagrdless of what Newmill achieved here. **Briareus** would have finished fourth of fifth but for falling at the last, his limitations essentially exposed as a 2-miler, but there could still be a high-class performance in him at around 2½m given his lightly-raced profile and how he shaped in the King George; ridden handily, he was at work to hold his position from the top of the hill, his departure forewarned as his jumping became ragged over the final 3 fences. **Twist Magic** has become something of an underachiever and was let down badly by his jumping here, making a series of mistakes from the seventh (well held when eventually falling 2 out), having proved mulish to post.

3949	**Weatherbys Champion Bumper**	2m110y
	(Standard Open NHF) (Gr 1) (1) (4, 5 and 6yo) £34,206	

2683*	DUNGUIB (IRE) *PhilipFenton,Ireland* 6-11-5 MrBTO'Connell	13/2	9/2	1
1694*	SOME PRESENT (IRE) *ThomasMullins,Ireland* 6-11-5			
	DNRussell..		10	2
			25/1	
3627*	RITE OF PASSAGE *DKWeld,Ireland* 5-11-5 PJSmullen	3	5/2f	¾ 3
2900*	Quel Esprit (FR) *WPMullins,Ireland* 5-11-5 RWalsh................		10/1	2 4
2751*	Morning Supreme (IRE) *WPMullins,Ireland* 6-10-12 MsKWalsh.....		25/1	14 5
3505*	Lead The Parade (IRE) *DKWeld,Ireland* 5-11-5 MrRPMcNamara.		40/1	2¾ 6
3009*	Cranky Corner *WPMullins,Ireland* 5-11-5 DJCondon...............		50/1	nk 7
2189*	Shinrock Paddy (IRE) *PaulNolan,Ireland* 5-11-5			
	MrBarryConnell..		12 10/1	2 8
2968*	Pepe Simo (IRE) *PFNicholls* 5-11-5 SamThomas		50/1	3¼ 9
3418⁴	Benbane Head (USA) *MKeighley* 5-11-5 WarrenMarston.........		100/1	hd 10
872*	Meath All Star *WPMullins,Ireland* 6-11-5 PaulTownend		12/1	1 11
2955⁴	Long Standard (IRE) *CFSwan,Ireland* 5-11-5 RichardHughes...		50/1	2¾ 12
3614*	Latin America (IRE) *NJGifford* 4-10-11 JayPemberton............		66/1	1½ 13
2758*	Red Harbour *PFNicholls* 5-11-5 LiamHeard		33/1	nk 14
2662*	Gagewell Flyer (IRE) *WPMullins,Ireland* 5-11-5 DJCasey		14/1	2 15
3486*	Sicilian Secret (IRE) *WPMullins,Ireland* 6-11-5 MrPWMullins....	13/2	9/1	13 16
3773*	Fennis Boy (IRE) *JohnJosephHanlon,Ireland* 5-11-5			
	SEDurack..		150/1	23 17
2402*	Henry King (IRE) *VRADartnall* 5-11-5 TimmyMurphy..............		20/1	1¾ 18
2934*	Abroad *JamesLeavy,Ireland* 5-11-5 JAHeffernan....................		66/1	5 19
3418²	Double Dash *GeorgeBaker* 5-11-5 AndrewTinkler..................		100/1	1¼ 20
3524*	Lightening Rod *MWEasterby* 4-10-11 MrOGreenall................		100/1	3 21
3186*	Cadspeed (FR) *WPMullins,Ireland* 6-11-5 EmmetMullins........		16/1	8 22
2690*	Bygones of Brid (IRE) *KarenMcLintock* 6-11-5 GLee		50/1	13 23
3030*	Quincia Des Obeaux (FR) *WPMullins,Ireland* 5-11-5			
	APMcCoy...		14 16/1	17 24

5.15race Mr Daniel Harnett 24ran 3m56.88

An impressive winner, who ran to one of the highest Timeform bumper ratings ever, and the form behind him probably shouldn't be underestimated even though several failed to live up to expectations, notably the 8-strong Willie Mullins team; it was a well-run affair and the first 4 pulled well clear, the first British-trained runner home only ninth. **Dunguib**, well backed late on, was one of the most impressive winners of this race in its 17-year history, not settling especially well early yet still travelling powerfully throughout and quickening decisively in the straight, staying on strongly to the line—this was a top-notch performance and, as a scopey, athletic sort, he looks to have an extremely bright future in novice hurdles next season. **Some Present**, by the same sire as the winner, was less experienced than that rival and did well to come through and chase him home, showing greenness still down the hill and taking time to pick up when ridden but staying on well towards the finish to take second close home; he may well progress further and will stay beyond 2m once sent over hurdles. **Rite of Passage** was all the rage beforehand and had every chance but was beaten on merit, ridden to challenge 3f out but having no answer to the winner's turn of foot in the straight; he has a future as a jumper but, given his pedigree and stable, he might also make his mark on the Flat. **Quel Esprit** emerged best of his stable's 8-strong contingent and was clear of the rest, showing himself a useful prospect, though having already won at 2½m he confirmed that stamina is his strong suit, doing his best work late on, lacking much in the way of a turn of foot. **Morning Supreme**, the one mare in the field, acquitted herself quite well despite failing to match her Downpatrick form—she enjoyed a soft lead until the winner went on, but soon had nothing left and faded late on. **Lead The Parade**, a better type than his stable companion Rite of Passage, didn't altogether take the eye in condition but ran respectably, particularly given he was left with plenty to do under his amateur, coming from the rear 4f out but unable to sustain his effort in the straight; he has the potential to make a decent novice hurdler next season. **Cranky Corner** couldn't build significantly on the form of his Fairyhouse win in this stronger race, held up well off the pace and staying on after 3f out but unable to land a blow; he's likely to benefit from more of a test of stamina. **Shinrock Paddy** was a long way below the form he showed when so impressive here in the autumn, racing second this time and seeming to tire after 3f out; he's still one of the better prospects for novice hurdling in this field. **Pepe Simo** emerged best of the small British-trained contingent and shaped a bit better than the result suggests too, as he was involved in scrimmaging at the top of the hill after travelling smoothly and took time to recover, closing 3f out but unable to sustain his effort in the straight; he has his quirks but a fair amount of ability and should make a hurdler next season. **Benbane Head** had raced on heavy going previously and left the impression this less testing ground didn't provide enough emphasis on stamina, behind when hampered at the top of the hill before staying on dourly to be nearest at the finish. **Meath All Star**'s looks don't match his pedigree and he had quite a hard race on this first start since the summer, running below his Cork form in the process, more patiently ridden this time but just staying on steadily when asked for his effort. **Long Strand** was one of the better types in the field but his form looked short of what was required and he could make little impression once shaken up down the hill after being patiently ridden; he has some potential as a longer-distance novice hurdler. **Latin America** rather belies his pedigree and, even though he didn't run up to his previous form in this much stronger race, he looked all about stamina in staying on steadily through beaten horses; he isn't the biggest and may struggle to make a major impact as a hurdler. **Red Harbour** failed to run near his previous form, moving into contention 5f out but flat out 3f out and weakening in the straight; the level of his previous form suggests he's likely to leave this behind in novice hurdles in the autumn. **Gagewell Flyer** was the best type in the field on looks but he didn't look the most straightforward, failing to settle early on then looking short of pace when asked to pick up and hanging badly right in the straight; he might be seen to better advantage with more experience under his belt. **Sicilian Secret**, who took a good hold and raced prominently, ran better than the distances indicate, still seeming in need of the experience when shaken up and, having been unable to quicken 3f out, eased a good deal late on;

he's not the most athletic to look at but can be expected to make an impact in maiden/novice hurdles in the autumn, with softer ground/longer trips likely to be in his favour. **Fennis Boy** is nothing much on looks, had plenty to find on form and was behind 4f out. **Henry King**, so impressive when beating Pepe Simo at Newbury, seemed to be making progress into contention 4f out after being dropped out but he didn't pick up and was soon eased right off; he may yet show himself the smart prospect he looked on his debut. **Abroad** isn't much on looks and his form didn't suggest he had much chance either, so it was little surprise he couldn't hold his position after 4f out, finishing well held. **Double Dash**, sweating and on his toes, was well placed until dropping out quickly 4f out, finishing well held; his form, which wouldn't have been good enough anyway, is on soft/heavy going. **Lightening Rod** was already very much on the retreat when involved in scrimmaging at the top of the hill, finishing well held. **Cadspeed** had raced on soft/heavy going previously and looked nothing like so effective in a competitive race on this less testing surface, quickly losing his place 5f out and finishing tailed off. **Bygones of Brid** had shown useful form on barely raceable ground on his second start but looked out of his depth in this company, well behind 4f out. **Quinola des Obeaux** had looked a smart prospect in winning both previous starts and clearly wasn't right here, racing freely but stopping quickly over 5f out and soon tailed off.

CHELTENHAM Thursday, Mar 12

3959 Ryanair Chase (Festival) (Gr 1) (1) (5yo+) £125,422   2m5f (17)

2817 6	IMPERIAL COMMANDER (IRE) NATwiston-Davies 8-11-10 PJBrennan	6/1	1
3441 *	VOY POR USTEDES (FR) AKing 8-11-10 RobertThornton	10/11 4/5f	2 2
3625 2	SCHINDLERS HUNT (IRE) DTHughes,Ireland 9-11-10 (t) PWFlood	22/1	¾ 3
3204 3	Tidal Bay (IRE) JHowardJohnson 8-11-10 DenisO'Regan	6 13/2	4½ 4
3441 2	Gwanako (FR) PFNicholls 6-11-10 RWalsh	16/1	1½ 5
2617 *	Monet's Garden (IRE) NGRichards 11-11-10 DJCondon	20/1	6 6
3509 5	Mister McGoldrick MrsSJSmith 12-11-10 DominicElsworth	40/1	3 7
3297 5	Knight Legend (IRE) MrsJHarrington,Ireland 10-11-10 (t) ADLeigh	100/1	17 8
2556 5	L'Antartique (FR) FerdyMurphy 9-11-10 GLee	33/1	pu
2817 pu	Our Vic (IRE) DEPipe 11-11-10 (b) TimmyMurphy	8 9/1	pu

2.40race Our Friends in the North 10ran 5m18.32

A couple ducking the fruitless task of taking on Master Minded in the Champion Chase and one who once harboured Gold Cup hopes fought out the finish to the fifth running of this in-between race, while a pair of top-class chasers with something to prove were also in the field—despite its Grade 1 status, this race is still very much in the shadow of both the Champion and Gold Cup, for all it's a high-class contest in its own right; it was the least well-run of the 3 races over the course and distance on this card, with the field still well grouped before 3 out as the pace really quickened, and the time was the slowest of the 3 too. **Imperial Commander** hadn't shaped so badly as the result suggested at Kempton and, impressing in appearance on this return from 2½ months off, he took a further step forward to resume winning ways under a well-judged ride, leading 6 out (always prominent) and quickening decisively 3 out, ridden out after a rare untidy leap at the last (jumped well otherwise); this was just his sixth start over fences (fourth win) and there is more to come, so it wouldn't be a surprise to see him develop into a Gold Cup contender in time—nearer to hand, he still holds a Grand National entry, though it wouldn't be a surprise if the Melling or the Bowl were chosen as alternative options for him at Aintree. **Voy Por Ustedes**, who typically looked very well, was a bit below his best as he fluffed his lines due to a rare jumping error, a bad mistake 4 out just as the race was about to take shape crucial to his chance, for he'd travelled strongly until then and had to be shaken up as the pace was quickening, lacking the pace to press the winner in the straight but battling on for second after the last; the Melling at Aintree is likely to give him the chance to gain compensation for the second year running. **Schindlers Hunt** didn't take the eye particularly but ran a fine race, the return to 21f suiting him well, making headway going well 3 out, ridden after the winner in the straight but unable to close and losing second close home; this looks his optimum trip nowadays and he'll presumably be back for the Melling at Aintree next month. **Tidal Bay** hasn't progressed quite as expected since he was so impressive in the Arkle last year and, as at Wetherby on his penultimate start, he ran rather a moody race, not especially fluent and losing his position after halfway, behind 4 out and not really applying himself (jockey did briefly accept matters) before running on well from the last; he is worth trying in headgear. **Gwanako**, again on his toes, ran well but simply isn't quite up to this class and, although he travelled well tracking the leaders, he was quickly beaten when the race developed after 3 out; he won the Topham at Aintree last spring, though whether he will be able to win it again off a much higher mark must be doubted, particularly after his unfortunate experience in the Grand Sefton. **Monet's Garden**, although he finished second in the 2006 Arkle, probably isn't ideally suited by this track and, sweating slightly, he ran below form after 3 months off, a mistake 3 out as he was making his effort meaning he could make little impression after; he may be seen to better advantage back at Aintree next, though his form last time hasn't stood up that well and he may not be quite the force he was. **Mister McGoldrick** had sprung a surprise in the Festival Plate last season but couldn't repeat the feat in this better race, close up to 4 out but left behind as the pace quickened at the next; overall, he's not the force he was. **Knight Legend**'s jumping proved his undoing again, blundering at the thirteenth and 3 out, soon beaten after the latter; he was tried in a first-time tongue strap, incidentally. **L'Antartique**, on just his second start of the season, ran no race at all and hinted at temperament yet again, never going well in rear, eventually pulled up before 4 out. **Our Vic** couldn't have looked in better shape for his fifth appearance in this race but, as on the first occasion, he was pulled up and has got plenty to prove at present—as at Kempton 2½ months earlier, he left the impression all wasn't well as he stopped quickly before 4 out.

```
3960      Ladbrokes World Hdle (Gr 1) (1) (4yo+) £148,226              3m (12)
3206*  BIG BUCK'S (FR) PFNicholls 6-11-10 RWalsh................ 13/2 6/1       1
3206²  PUNCHESTOWNS (IRE) NJHenderson 6-11-10 BJGeraghty ..... 3 10/3  1¾  2
3358²  POWERSTATION (IRE) EamonO'Connell,Ireland 9-11-10              17   3
          AJMcNamara................................................ 25/1
3446*  Kasbah Bliss (FR) FDoumen,France 7-11-10 CPieux........ 11/10 10/11  1¾  4
          Mighty Man (FR) HDDaly 9-11-10 SamThomas............... 28/1    5   5
3181²  Whatuthink (IRE) OliverMcKiernan,Ireland 7-11-10 (b)                hd  6
          DNRussell................................................ 100/1
2755⁵  Mobaasher (USA) PFNicholls 6-11-10 (b+t) ChristianWilliams..... 33/1   4½  7
3206⁶  Blazing Bailey AKing 7-11-10 (b) RobertThornton ........... 28/1   2¼  8
3206³  Fair Along (GER) PJHobbs 7-11-10 RichardJohnson.......... 12 14/1  1¾  9
3206⁵  No Refuge (IRE) JHowardJohnson 9-11-10 DenisO'Regan....... 100/1 4½ 10
3206   Pettifour (IRE) NATwiston-Davies 7-11-10 PJBrennan ........ 66/1   5  11
3450²  Tazbar (IRE) KGReveley 7-11-10 JamesReveley ............. 33/1  16  12
3181³  Shakervilz (FR) WPMullins,Ireland 6-11-10 PaulTownend...... 50/1 3¾ 13
3611⁵  Afsoun (FR) NJHenderson 7-11-10 DominicElsworth ......... 100/1 27 14
3.20race The Stewart Family 14ran 5m56.47
```

An excellent renewal of the staying hurdlers' championship, one which has been dominated in recent years by the now-retired Inglis Drever, though the latter would have been hard pushed to beat the first 2 here even if at the very top of his game—Big Buck's and Punchestowns will presumably have their attentions turned to chasing soon, but they're both top-notch performers who'll set a very high standard if kept to this sphere; the pace steadied slightly mid-race, but it was essentially a good one and stamina was certainly tested as things began to take shape before 2 out, with the odds-on favourite seemingly found wanting on that score. **Big Buck's** came to these shores with a huge reputation and it's now absolutely clear why, this his sixth win from 9 completed starts for present connections, whose decision to revert him to hurdles this season has proved a masterstroke—he'll continue to take all the beating if kept to this sphere, though he'd clearly also be well worth his place in the top staying chases next winter should the decision be made to send him back over fences; travelling strongly under restraint, he was produced with a well-timed challenge at the last and, although bungling that flight, always seemed to be getting the best of things on the run-in despite idling a shade, in the process reversing placings from race 3206 off 8 lb worse terms. **Punchestowns**, who looked very well, emerged with plenty of credit despite failing to take advantage of an 8 lb pull in the weights with Big Buck's from their meeting in race 3206, not always fluent (no serious errors) yet travelling strongly in touch from halfway, leading before 2 out but unable to withstand the winner's strong finish despite that rival's blunder at the last; he pulled well clear of the remainder and is clearly a top-notch hurdler, though it wouldn't be a surprise if fences are on the agenda for 2009/10—he appeals as the type to do equally well in that sphere. **Powerstation** can boast an excellent record at this track—placed on all 5 starts here now—and he bounced back from his Clonmel flop with a career-best effort, improving from mid-division (mistake 3 out) to challenge from 2 out, sticking to his task well thereafter, regaining third from the last. **Kasbah Bliss** didn't have quite the chance that the one-sided betting market suggested but, as when only fifth in the 2007 renewal of this race, he essentially shaped as if this trip stretched his stamina in a well-run affair, making steady headway under a patient ride (taken wide virtually throughout) but unable to sustain his effort on the long run to the last, even losing third on the run-in; it's worth noting that his second place in the 2008 renewal came on the Old Course (due to Wednesday's abandonment that year) and it's possible that the New Course doesn't suit him ideally. **Mighty Man**, a top-class staying hurdler (placed in 2006 and 2007 renewals of this race), had been sidelined for nearly 2 years since breaking down badly at Punchestown and shaped as if retaining much of his ability on this unexpected comeback, particularly as he looked beforehand as if the run would put him spot on, keeping on steadily after racing in touch for much of the way (mistake eighth); he's unbeaten in 3 starts at Aintree and will presumably now bid for a third win in the Liverpool Hurdle on the opening day of that track's 3-day meeting next month—he'd be far from a forlorn hope there, though place prospects could well be the best he could hope for if the big 2 here reoppose. **Whatuthink** is a likeable sort but seems fully exposed now, even at this sort of trip, and he did about as well as could be expected in the face of a stiff task, racing with plenty of zest at the head of affairs in first-time blinkers and then sticking to his task pretty well once headed after a mistake 3 out. **Mobaasher**, returning from 12 weeks off, looked very well beforehand but failed to make much of an impact in the race itself (refitted with blinkers), patiently ridden as usual and soon done with once niggled after 3 out; he'll presumably be switched to fences in 2009/10, though could have temperament issues in that sphere. **Blazing Bailey** simply doesn't seem the force of old this season and, not helped by a couple of mid-race mistakes, he was badly outpaced soon after the third last; connections are reportedly keen to try him over fences, but he's not an obvious chasing type on looks and it's far from certain that such a switch will revitalise him in 2009/10. **Fair Along** was entitled to finish in the frame judged on his form against each of the first 3 earlier in the season but, for whatever reason, he turned in a rare below-par effort—it's possible he was unsuited by being unable to lead (tracked pace this time) but such tactics haven't always been a necessity in the past and he probably just had an off-day, fading from before 2 out. **No Refuge** isn't up to this class (only thirteenth in 2006 renewal) but he still didn't run much of a race, never a factor after hitting the first and detached some way out. **Pettifour** has rather struggled in good company since his winning reappearance and clearly might not be up to this class, though it's worth noting that he again went out pretty quickly here—soon not persevered with after a mistake 3 out—so there must be a chance he's got some sort of problem at present; he remains an exciting novice chase prospect for 2009/10 despite those concerns. **Tazbar** isn't quite up to this class but, as when a course-and-distance fifth under top weight behind Big Buck's back in January, he spoiled his chance with a very lazy display (detached from halfway) and could do with trying in headgear on this evidence. **Shakervilz** was tackling much stronger company than in Ireland this winter and ultimately finished well held, but he actually shaped better than plenty who finished in front of him, travelling well up with the pace until those exertions took their toll from 2 out; he should continue to give a good account back in calmer waters. **Afsoun** remains very difficult to place and ruined any chance he had of staying this longer trip by getting stirred up beforehand (something he's done before), then failing to settle under a patient ride (beaten by 3 out).

CHELTENHAM Friday, Mar 13

3969 JCB Triumph Hdle (Gr 1) (1) (4yo) £68,412   2m1f (8)

3119¹	ZAYNAR (FR) *NJ*Henderson 4-11-0 (s) BJGeraghty 9/2 11/2		1
3205¹	WALKON (FR) *A*King 4-11-0 RobertThornton.................... 9/2 4/1		¾ 2
3479³	MOURAD (IRE) *WP*Mullins,*Ireland* 4-11-0 RWalsh 14/1		2¾ 3
2881*	Starluck (IRE) *A*Fleming 4-11-0 TimmyMurphy............... 6 5/1		3½ 4
3588*	Trenchant *A*King 4-11-0 WayneHutchinson................... 28/1		3 5
3205²	Reve de Sivola (FR) *Nick*Williams 4-11-0 DarylJacob............ 20/1		1¼ 6
3205³	Simarian (IRE) *Evan*Williams 4-11-0 DonalFahy.............. 40/1		13 7
1439*	Tyrrells Wood (IRE) *TG*Mills 4-11-0 JamieMoore............... 66/1		3¾ 8
3479*	Jumbo Rio (IRE) *EJ*O'Grady,*Ireland* 4-11-0 AJMcNamara ... 12 11/1		¾ 9
3059²	Tharawaat (FR) *G*Elliott,*Ireland* 4-11-0 DNRussell................ 40/1		3¾ 10
3309*	Master of Arts (USA) *DE*Pipe 4-11-0 TomScudamore...... 6 17/2		3¾ 11
2878	Just Rob *Ian*Williams 4-11-0 DavidDennis 150/1		2½ 12
3191*	Silk Drum (IRE) *J*HowardJohnson 4-11-0 DenisO'Regan........ 25/1		1¼ 13
3448*	Stow *Miss*VenetiaWilliams 4-11-0 SamThomas................ 50/1		2¼ 14
3496⁴	Maidstone Mixture (FR) *Paul*Murphy 4-11-0 RichardMcGrath 250/1		23 15
2862*	Lethal Weapon (IRE) *C*Roche,*Ireland* 4-11-0 APMcCoy 14 17/2		6 16
3470¹	Art Sleuth (USA) *WP*Mullins,*Ireland* 4-11-0 (t) PaulTownend 66/1		19 17
3479²	Ebadiyan (IRE) *Patrick*OBrady,*Ireland* 4-11-0 JCullen.............. 17/2 8/1		ro

1.30race Men In Our Position 18ran 4m03.91

A stronger race than the Supreme earlier in the week and right up with the best Triumphs, potentially a springboard to the top table for several of the principals, with recent trends much more encouraging for juveniles going on to make the grade as 5-y-o's—Binocular, Celestial Halo and Katchit have all made the transition; the field was bunched through the early stages but stamina and ability was tested as the long-time market principals came to the fore, with the winner seeming to do no more than was required. **Zaynar** stamped himself as the best juvenile around as he confirmed Newbury superiority over Walkon off 7 lb worse terms and took his unbeaten record to 3, looking the type who'll follow the winners of the last 3 years and hold his own against the best in open company; whilst he'll stay beyond 2m he's by no means slow given a test at this trip, jumping slickly this time with cheekpieces on and getting to the front on the bridle 2 out, shrugging off a baulk at that flight and essentially waiting for something to come at him, always finding enough up the hill and probably having a bit in reserve. **Walkon** showed his all, which might not have been the case with the other 3 in the frame, but he's established himself as a smart hurdler nevertheless, one whose attitude will continue to stand him in good stead, having to work to get into a challenging position and sustaining it up the hill; he seems likely to head to Aintree next, where Zaynar reportedly won't be in opposition. **Mourad** emerged as the best Irish-trained juvenile seen out so far this season, with the stiff test at the trip right up his street—indeed, if anything, it failed to get to the very bottom of him, bounding up the hill having crept into things and been aksed for full effort only after bungling the last; there's better still to come from him at some stage, possibly when tried over further. **Starluck** has still to have his limitations exposed, failing for stamina as much as anything as he met with this first defeat over hurdles, and he looks the one to beat at Aintree with Zaynar reportedly staying away, looming upsides that rival going easily turning in and showing a deal more speed than Walkon (who's also bound for Aintree). **Trenchant** is firmly established as a useful juvenile after 4 runs, this another advance from Kempton, but he showed a temperamental side on the Flat and looked one to have reservations about as he laboured in rear for a long way, never threatening to get involved, even allowing for the fact that he could be ideally suited by more of a stamina test in top company. **Reve de Sivola** could have reached his ceiling at 2m now, producing a similar effort to last time as he was ridden more positively, encountering different ground and making a couple of early mistakes, but essentially seeming beaten for ability after stumbling briefly turning in; his trainer has already outlined plans to campaign towards the Baring Bingham next season, but he's built to make a chaser one day. **Simarian** reiterated his need for further and, compounded by conditions, he was struggling in rear by halfway before running through rivals late. **Tyrrells Wood**, fit from the Flat, ran to a similarly fairly useful level as he produced in that sphere, deserving credit for one so inexperienced over hurdles and better may still come (mistake first), losing touch with the principals only in the straight; he'll set a good standard under a penalty if found an opportunity in an ordinary juvenile in the final weeks of the season. **Jumbo Rio** was closely matched with the third on previous efforts and still has mileage in him, likely to be suited by an easier 2m but possibly amiss to go out as quickly as he did, left in front going well approaching 2 out but soon folding following an awkward jump there (baulked winner). **Tharawaat** had already had his limitations exposed by the best juveniles in Ireland but still ran below form, this stiff test possibly telling after he'd been in touch turning in. **Master of Arts** may have stamina issues at a testing 2m but this proved inconclusive, failing the test on jumping grounds, rarely fluent and never any closer than mid-division; his Doncaster defeat of Copper Bleu had been boosted by that one's performance here earlier in the week. **Just Rob** has been proven out of his depth in graded company, his previous defeat of Indian Groom and Ski Sunday probably worth a good deal less than it might look on paper now. **Silk Drum** rather had his hand forced into taking up this stiff test, a mark of 145 for the Fred Winter brutal, but he ran below form even so, weakening fully 3 out (had raced keenly); he's unlikely to be easy to place in the short term. **Stow** has been put in his place each time he's taken on useful opposition, a blunder at the fifth compounding the severity of this task; his handicap mark looks to leave little room for manoeuvre too. **Maidstone Mixture** fortunately didn't hinder the realistic contenders, as he'd done when a rank outsider in the St Leger. **Lethal Weapon**, who'd shown signs of quirkiness for all he'd gone unbeaten previously, clearly had some sort of an issue here—be it physical or temperamental—and had already dropped out before making his second mistake at the fifth; it's also possibly significant that he'd been off for nearly 3 months. **Art Sleuth** had some gap to bridge on form, though there could be another issue for him to have run this badly (tongue tied again), always in rear; whilst he'd raced on heavy going over hurdles previously, his Flat form suggests this less testing surface shouldn't have been a problem. **Ebadiyan**'s Leopardstown running last time generally stood up through others but he blotted his record badly, winding things up from the front going down the hill only to cock his jaw and run out at the second last; he'd also made a mistake at the fourth.

3971 Albert Bartlett Nov Hdle (Spa) (Gr) (1) (4yo+) £57,010 3m (12)

3237²	WEAPON'S AMNESTY (IRE) *CharlesByrnes,Ireland* 6-11-7		1
	DNRussell	9 8/1	
3289⁵	PRIDE OF DULCOTE (FR) *PFNicholls* 6-11-7 RWalsh	3/1f	½ 2
3195⁵	THE MIDNIGHT CLUB (IRE) *WPMullins,Ireland* 8-11-7		2 3
	EmmetMullins	16 14/1	
3212¹	On Raglan Road (IRE) *JHowardJohnson* 6-11-7 *DenisO'Regan* .	12 9/1	5 4
3212¹	Cape Tribulation *JMJefferson* 5-11-7 PhilKinsella	10/3 4/1	3 5
3212ᴾᵁ	Midnight Sail *AKing* 6-11-7 WayneHutchinson	100/1	5 6
3074¹	Browns Baily (IRE) *MFMorris,Ireland* 7-11-7 NPMadden	12 11/1	10 7
3449²	Thetwincamdrift (IRE) *AKing* 7-11-7 RobertThornton	16/1	2¼ 8
3534¹	On The Way Out (IRE) *JohnEKiely,Ireland* 6-11-7 TomDoyle	33/1	dist 9
3112²	Bally Sands (IRE) *RMathew* 5-11-7 MattyRoe	100/1	5 10
2915³	Toby Belch (IRE) *HDDaly* 6-11-7 AndrewTinkler	80/1	27 11
3442²	Chariot Charger (IRE) *MissECLavelle* 5-11-7 JackDoyle	33/1	20 12
3181*	Alpha Ridge (IRE) *PaulNolan,Ireland* 7-11-7 (t) APCawley	15/2	pu
3254*	Den of Iniquity *CarlLlewellyn* 8-11-7 PJBrennan	25/1	pu
3212ᴾᵁ	Diablo (IRE) *NATwiston-Davies* 7-11-7 (t) DavidEngland	66/1	pu
3380²	Picture In The Sky (IRE) *MKeighley* 8-11-7 (b) WarrenMarston	100/1	pu
3481²	Western Charmer (IRE) *DTHughes,Ireland* 7-11-7 PWFlood	25/1	pu

2.40race Gigginstown House Stud 17ran 5m59.84

A race with a good deal more depth that looked likely beforehand, with the winner and third both raising their game as they drew away with one who already looked up to the standard of previous renewals, Weapon's Amnesty having more in reserve. **Weapon's Amnesty** had earned his place in this field, having won a graded event in the mud in Ireland and emerged as the best horse when runner-up in another, but his smart performance here was another marked improvement and, what's more, it still looks by no means his limit, coming there easily and idling markedly after soon going 2 lengths clear from the last; likely to stay long distances, he'll reportedly go over fences next season and looks an exciting prospect; this was a first Cheltenham winner for his trainer, incidentally, after saddling the runner-up in this contest on 2 of the previous 3 years. **Pride of Dulcote**, ante-post favourite for this for much of the winter, underlined his status as a smart novice but, after being brought along mainly in less competitive events, he appeared to have his limitations exposed too, travelling smoothly into a narrow lead approaching 2 out but hanging left initially when driven and soon brushed aside as he hit the last, finishing so close to the winner only by virtue of that one's idling. **The Midnight Club**'s progress has been rapid since he finished down the field in a bumper for another yard last summer and this was another big step forward, for all he met with his first defeat for this stable; he's on the lean side, rather like the winner, but looks just the type who'll do well in long-distance chases all the same (winning pointer) and looked a real stayer here, taking an eternity to get going on this less testing ground, hanging left in the straight too. **On Raglan Road** is a useful novice, well established in graded company now, but his limitations have been there to see too, this another occasion after he'd raced handily and had every chance early in the straight, finding less than seemed likely. **Cape Tribulation** looked to have the beating of On Raglan Road from Doncaster and should make more of an impact at Aintree, be it at 2½m or 3m, just about matching the runner-up as the pair moved on powerfully after 3 out but failing to get up the hill. **Midnight Sail** hadn't given his running at Doncaster and his second shot at graded company proved more fruitful, showing the useful level of form he had in bumpers, still very much on the heels of the principals 2 out. **Browns Baily** is a useful sort but he's come up short when asked to take on the best, one of the first off the bridle here having not always been fluent and, whilst digging in, he was soon left behind 2 out. **Thetwincamdrift** underlined the relative weakness of his Grade 2 placing at Haydock, never able to get on terms here for all he probably ran creditably on form. **On The Way Out**'s hurdles wins have been in the mud but he's fully effective under these less testing conditions and, despite standing out in terms of well-being beforehand, he ran no sort of race following his Punchestown fall, a mistake at the eighth not helping. **Bally Sands** should have little trouble winning ordinary novices, his form at a lower level standing up well, but this was an unrealistic task and he was one of the first beaten going to 3 out; he was one of the better sorts on looks, the type who should make a chaser. **Toby Belch**'s jumping isn't yet assured and it failed to stand up at all to this test after 2½ months off, dropping out tamely going to 3 out. **Chariot Charger** looked worth his place in graded company, on potential if not quite proven form, and shouldn't necessarily be judged on this as he went from travelling easily held up to labouring in a matter of strides at the top of the hill, leaving the impression something was amiss. **Alpha Ridge**'s form is Ireland stands up, Whatuthink doing his bit for it in the World Hurdle, the obvious conclusion here being that he possibly isn't the same horse away from testing ground, at work to keep his lead from early on the second circuit and already headed when squeezed out after the third last. **Den of Iniquity**'s fragility is plain to see and he seemed to go wrong again when leading the field towards 2 out, still to be asked for his effort too (had made running). **Diablo** looks to have lost the plot, becoming detached from halfway here even allowing for the fact this was a stiff task. **Picture In The Sky** proved just as idle in headgear, acknowledging the harshness of his task, making mistakes too. **Western Charmer** evidently wasn't right as he dropped through the field from the seventh; he looks held by Ireland's best novices but has the potential to do better over fences—indeed, he was the paddock pick here.

3972 totesport Cheltenham Gold Cup Chase (Gr 1) 3¼m110y (22)
(1) (5yo+) £270,798

2817*	KAUTO STAR (FR) *PFNicholls* 9-11-10 (t) RWalsh 13/8 7/4f 1
3401²	DENMAN (IRE) *PFNicholls* 9-11-10 SamThomas 13/2 7/1 13 2
2925*	EXOTIC DANCER (FR) *JonjoO'Neill* 9-11-10 (s) APMcCoy 8/1 2½ 3
3484*	Neptune Collonges (FR) *PFNicholls* 8-11-10 ChristianWilliams ... 8 15/2 6 4
2440⁵	My Will (FR) *PFNicholls* 9-11-10 NickScholfield 100/1 2 5
3204 pu	Roll Along (IRE) *CarlLlewellyn* 9-11-10 GLee .... 40/1 nk 6
2543	Barbers Shop *NJHenderson* 7-11-10 BJGeraghty 11 10/1 9 7
3401*	Madison du Berlais (FR) *DEPipe* 8-11-10 (s) TomScudamore 10/1 10 8
3401³	Albertas Run (IRE) *JonjoO'Neill* 8-11-10 DominicElsworth 14/1 5 9
2440	Knowhere (IRE) *NATwiston-Davies* 9-11-10 PJBrennan 100/1 14 10
4788 pu	Cerium (FR) *PaulMurphy* 8-11-10 KeithMercer 300/1 1¾ 11
2817⁵	Air Force One (GER) *CJMann* 7-11-10 NoelFehily 25 16/1 5 12
3204⁴	Star de Mohaison (FR) *PFNicholls* 8-11-10 (t) TimmyMurphy 20/1 2¾ 13
3447³	Miko de Beauchene (FR) *RH&MrsSAlner* 9-11-10 AndrewThornton .... 150/1 f
3204²	Halcon Genelardais (FR) *AKing* 9-11-10 (s) RobertThornton ...... 40/1 pu
3204 pu	Snoopy Loopy (IRE) *PBowen* 11-11-10 (b) SEDurack .... 66/1 pu

3.20race Mr Clive D. Smith 16ran 6m44.70

A Cheltenham Gold Cup that will live long in the memory, one of the best for many a year, with the winner producing an outstanding performance, arguably the best in this race since the days of Arkle, but one supported by good efforts from a strong field behind him (the third produced an effort that would have been good enough to win several recent runnings), the majority running some sort of race and none having a hard-luck story; the pace was not that strong early on but built as the race developed, with plenty still in contention 4 out before the winner asserted into the straight; the form has a really solid look to it, though the fifth and sixth might be marginally flattered by the run of things; 4 of the first 5 were trained by Paul Nicholls, who clearly deserves much credit, especially for getting Denman back after his effort at Kempton. **Kauto Star**, the outstanding chaser of his generation, produced one of his very best performances in the blue riband of the sport, arguably the best in this race since the days of Arkle, laying to rest questions raised by his defeat here last year and ending once and for all any doubt about his place among the greats; he travelled superbly well (always handy), jumping well throughout, and quickened clear of Denman off the home turn having taken over after 3 out, running on strongly kept up to his work; even if this proves to be his last run of a curtailed campaign, he has shown himself still very much the one to beat in the top races next season. **Denman**, as he can, didn't take the eye beforehand but ran a cracker given his less than ideal preparation, not nearly so forcefully ridden this year as when successful in 2008 but always handy, jumping superbly as usual, ridden 4 out and every chance when the winner went on, one paced in the straight, running only a little below his best; he clearly retains all his ability and, while there might not be much left for him this season, he will hopefully be back in a year's time after a trouble-free build-up, when the 'decider' between the first 2 should be something to see. **Exotic Dancer** was placed in the race for the second time, showing himself at least as good as ever, much more patiently ridden than the other principals, coming steadily through from the rear 5 out having made a few minor mistakes, ridden after 3 out and keeping on without being able to land a blow; his Aintree record is a little mixed, though he won the Bowl in 2007 and would likely be a leading contender if taking his chance in that again next month (also holds a Grand National entry and reportedly may take his chance in that). **Neptune Collonges** ran a fine race but is unfortunate to be around in such a strong era for staying chasers and his best wasn't good enough as, having made much of the running, he was ridden after a mistake 4 out (also mistake eighth) and one paced once headed at the next; he'll presumably be back to Punchestown for the Gold Cup there at the end of the season, when in the absence of the first 3 here he'll hold a good chance of another Grade 1 success; he's thoroughly likeable. **My Will**, sweating slightly and not taking the eye particularly on his first start since the Henessy, hadn't done himself justice in the 2007 Gold Cup but rewarded connections decision to sidestep the William Hill Trophy on Tuesday with a career-best effort this time, in the process turning in a first-rate Grand National trial, for which he already looked the pick of the weights and he will surely go to Aintree with a favourite's chance—his solid jumping, abundant experience and ability to travel well enhancing his prospects there (also stays well); held up, he still had plenty to do 4 out but stayed on strongly in the straight and was nearest at the finish. **Roll Along** was about the pick of the paddock (albeit sweated up later in preliminaries) and he ran above himself, held up early (mistake eighth), making some ground 4 out but no impression down the hill before staying on late; like the third and fifth he holds a Grand National entry, though whether his temperament will stand up to the demands of the build-up to that race is in some doubt, whilst he won't look quite so well handicapped as the fifth. **Barbers Shop**, runner-up in both the Jewson and the Paddy Power on previous visits here, ran a cracking race upped in class despite his stamina seeming to give out late on—the Ryanair will probably be a better option for future Festivals; soon tracking the leaders, he was going well when making a mistake 4 out and also hit the next, weakening after. **Madison du Berlais** was less forcefully ridden than when beating the runner-up at Kempton and ran a little disappointingly, niggled after a mistake at the eleventh having raced close up, losing his place at the fourteenth and behind 4 out; the Kempton form remains hard to weigh up, though probably isn't much in advance of his Hennessy form. **Albertas Run** shaped better than he had behind

Madison du Berlais at Kempton but was still well below his King George form, moving into a prominent position 4 out but ridden and tapped for foot down the hill, weakening in the straight; he should stay beyond 25f. **Knowhere**, as he had the year before, completed despite a sloppy round of jumping, struggling early on the final circuit; he went on to run in the Grand National last year, unseating at second Valentine's when still well in contention (unseated early in 2007), and will presumably be back to try and make it third time lucky next month. **Cerium**, sold from Paul Nicholls for £18,000 last May, was a smart chaser in his prime but well out of his depth here and completed in his own time; he probably stays 3m and acts on soft going. **Air Force One** looked very well on his first start in 10 weeks but he was again found wanting at the highest level, in touch but ridden at the sixteenth and weakening when making a mistake at the eighteenth; he's still young enough to make an impact in top handicaps when he's back on song, but he simply doesn't look up to this class. **Star de Mohaison**, who looked very well and was on his toes, had missed the William Hill Trophy earlier at the meeting due to the ground and, given his record here, didn't look a forlorn hope of making the frame in this but perhaps his gruelling race last time had left its mark, for after racing in mid-division he was asked for his effort 5 out but could make little impression and was eased right off. **Miko de Beauchene** faced an insufficient test of stamina, plus a stiff task into the bargain, and he began to struggle at the fifteenth, out of contention when falling 4 out; like many of these he holds a Grand National entry and has the size to take to those fences, though connections might have hoped for a better prep run. **Halcon Genelardais** was tried in cheekpieces and ran a sour race (as he'd done when blinkered for the 2007 renewal), losing interest after a mistake at the seventh and well behind when pulled up before the thirteenth; he's been a splendid servant over the years but has had a number of hard races and it's possible he's starting to remember them. **Snoopy Loopy** has had a remarkable season but his limitations have been very much exposed on his last 3 starts and, not taking the eye particularly, he raced up with the pace for a circuit but lost his position and was soon flat out with a slow jump at the thirteenth, behind when pulled up 5 out; he holds a Grand National entry but he doesn't appeal as a likely type for those demanding fences.

AINTREE Friday, Apr 3

4367 John Smith's Melling Chase (Gr 1) (1) 2½m (16)
(5yo+) £114,020

3959 2	VOY POR USTEDES (FR) *AKing* 8-11-10 RobertThornton	11/8f	1
3959 3	SCHINDLERS HUNT (IRE) *DTHughes,Ireland* 9-11-10 (t) PWFlood	14 16/1	hd 2
3590 *	NACARAT (FR) *TRGeorge* 8-11-10 APMcCoy	7/2 4/1	4½ 3
3946 5	Scotirish (IRE) *WPMullins,Ireland* 8-11-10 RWalsh	16 14/1	3 4
3959 4	Tidal Bay (IRE) *JHowardJohnson* 8-11-10 DenisO'Regan	5 4/1	14 5
3946 4	Newmill (IRE) *JohnJosephMurphy,Ireland* 11-11-10 RMPower	50/1	10 6
3946 3	Petit Robin (FR) *NJHenderson* 6-11-10 BJGeraghty	9/1	19 7
3946 f	Briareus *AMBalding* 9-11-10 PJBrennan	25/1	pu
3743	Natal (FR) *PRNicholls* 8-11-10 (t) NickScholfield	100/1	pu
3461	Takeroc (FR) *PFNicholls* 6-11-10 ChristianWilliams	50/1	pu

3.10race Sir Robert Ogden 10ran 5m01.90

The first running in 6 years where both the Ryanair and Champion Chase winners have stayed away but standards were just about upheld by the placed horses from the former, who were locked in an sustained duel after finally getting to the front-running Nacarat, his gallop having soon strung the field out and made for a real test of jumping. **Voy Por Ustedes** put the Ryanair behind him as he followed up last year's success, having to battle hard to confirm superiority over the runner-up after another uncharacteristic mistake at a high-pressure point, this time 5 out, not quite at his sparkling best but showing determination nevertheless to get on top well after the last; he'll presumably follow a similar path to this season in 2009/10, with another crack at the King George worthwhile. **Schindlers Hunt** got even closer to Voy Por Ustedes than he had at Cheltenham, and a cleaner round of jumping would probably have seen him prevail, making 3 mistakes of note, notably at the second last as he went after Nacarat, leading going into the last only to be worn down; he gives the impression there's a top-class performance in him when it all comes together. **Nacarat** underlined the extent of his rise this season taking on some of the best around, essentially beaten for ability after looking to have got away from his pursuers with a bold leap 4 out, but cementing his high-class status nevertheless, sticking to his task for all 2 proved stronger from the last; he'll reportedly target the King George next season, and, whilst that will prove a stiffer test again, he's by no means fully exposed. **Scotsirish**'s limitations had appeared exposed at Cheltenham, and, acknowledging the longer trip here, there's a chance his proximity flattered him a shade, sitting out much of the race under a patient ride, merely closing up late on horses who'd been battling. **Tidal Bay** is wasting his talent, producing yet another reluctant performance here, seeming to lose interest after being tightened up at the ninth, hard work from then on and dropping out by the fourth last; he's best treated with caution. **Newmill**'s Cheltenham effort remains a standout in his recent form, ridden in similar fashion here but failing to stand up to the jumping test. **Petit Robin** didn't jump so well as he had at Cheltenham, his worst mistake 3 out putting paid to his chance, but 2m is probably his trip in any case, flagging badly by the second last.

Briareus struggled 3 weeks on from Cheltenham, a mistake at the ninth putting him on the back foot, behind when pulled up after 4 out. **Natal** has had a miserable season, trailing throughout here. **Takeroc**'s season has derailed badly since Christmas, his jumping letting him down here, not that he had a realistic chance against the principals in any case.

AINTREE Saturday, Apr 4

4374 John Smith's Aintree Hdle (Gr 1) (1) (4yo+) £96,917   2½m (11)

3469 *	SOLWHIT (FR) *CharlesByrnes,Ireland* 5-11-7 DNRussell 6/1	1
4087 *	FIVEFORTHREE (IRE) *WPMullins,Ireland* 7-11-7 PaulTownend .. 8 7/1	½ 2
3935²	UNITED (GER) *MrsLWadham* 8-11-0 DominicElsworth 28/1	3 3
4467 *	Al Eile (IRE) *JohnQueally,Ireland* 9-11-7 TimmyMurphy 9/2 4/11	2¾ 4
3501 *	Catch Me (GER) *EJO'Grady,Ireland* 7-11-7 AJMcNamara 9/2 13/2	1 5
3933	Whiteoak (IRE) *DMcCain,Jnr* 6-11-0 JasonMaguire 16/1	10 6
4352⁶	Hills of Aran *WKGoldsworthy* 7-11-7 JamieMoore 66/1	2½ 7
3933	Blue Bajan (IRE) *AndrewTurnell* 7-11-7 GLee 40/1	2¼ 8
3933	Hardy Eustace (IRE) *DTHughes,Ireland* 12-11-7 (v+t) PWFlood..... 40/1	13 9
3933	Jered (IRE) *NMeade,Ireland* 7-11-7 APMcCoy 8/1	2 10
3933²	Celestial Halo (IRE) *PFNicholls* 5-11-7 (t) RWalsh 4 9/2	3¼ 11
3933⁶	Katchit (IRE) *AKing* 6-11-7 RobertThornton 10/1	½ 12
3461	Songe (FR) *CELongsdon* 5-11-7 TomSiddall 150/1	1 13
3947	Franchoek (IRE) *AKing* 5-11-7 BJGeraghty 40/1	10 14
4157³	Cybergenic (FR) *PaulMurphy* 11-11-7 KeithMercer 200/1	pu
3933¹	Othermix (FR) *TRGeorge* 5-11-7 PJBrennan............................. 100/1	pu

2.50race Top Of The Hill Syndicate 16ran 5m00.25

A markedly bigger field than is the norm, but the depth didn't materialise as the majority of those who'd been to Cheltenham failed to fire in a race dominated by Irish horses in the end (provided 4 of the 5 who drew clear), though the front 2 are lightly raced and have the potential to go further yet; a slower gallop than in the earlier novice made for something of a test of speed, plenty still on the bridle 3 out. **Solwhit** took his next step up the ladder as he gained his fifth success from 7 starts over hurdles, establishing himself as a very smart hurdler, also underlining that he's not dependent on soft/heavy ground, and, as such, is likely to prove a force at Punchestown, where he won a 4-y-o event in 2008; he's not the most robust but soon put a bad mistake 4 out behind him, coming there on the bridle and battling back to overhaul the second on the run-in, the longer trip no issue. **Fiveforthree** will presumably renew rivalry with the winner at Punchestown given how little racing he's had this season, and he's improved further on this evidence, producing a very smart performance despite reportedly losing a hind shoe at some stage, looking likely to win as he came there strongly and took a narrow advantage after the last; he's still unexposed beyond 2½m, and, given his size, looks a fine prospect for novice chasing. **United** has her limitations, but she's smart nevertheless and has enjoyed another excellent season, placed in graded events at both Cheltenham and Aintree since her 2 wins, always prominent and squeezed out going to the last here, which brought an error, battling back past the fourth then, though beaten on merit by the first 2. **Al Eile**, successful on the Flat in February, had been prevented by injury from running over hurdles this season, ruled out of the entire campaign at one point, and wasn't quite at his best in a race he'd won 3 times previously, threatening plenty as he came there up the inner 3 out (had made mistake sixth) but unable to sustain his challenge from the last; he hasn't been asked to race beyond Aintree in the past but may go to Punchestown this time given how light his campaign has been. **Catch Me** isn't dependent on testing ground as such, but in top company he could well be vulnerable to something with more speed away from such conditions, that certainly looking the case in this falsely-run race after he'd held a chance 2 out. Whiteoak has failed to fire at the 2 big Festivals, improving to hold some chance going to the second last here but unable to sustain her effort, despite having form at this trip last season. **Hills of Aran** ran as he had in the face of another stiff task 2 days previously, battling without being able to show his all after a busy period. **Blue Bajan** is a 2-miler essentially, his effort turning in unsurprisingly short-lived, though it's unclear whether he's at his best at present, too, starting out more in touch than usual only to drop to rear as he jumped with no great fluency. **Hardy Eustace** isn't so reliable as he once was, this one of his lesser efforts after typically racing to the fore. **Jered** may prove best at 2m, still going strongly turning in, though whilst he jumped better on the whole than at Cheltenham he again gave cause for concern, making a real mess of 3 out as things were beginning to get serious. **Celestial Halo** remains unexposed beyond 2m, this clearly coming too soon after a gruelling race at Cheltenham as he went out tamely turning in; he's hard as nails as a rule, and his Champion Hurdle form remains in advance of what the principals here achieved. Katchit found it all hard work after being tightened up with a circuit to race, all possibly not well as he lost his place by 5 out; he'd promised to be suited by 2½m, and could be worth trying in headgear. Songe has run poorly on both starts since his win, he another to do so after being hampered with a circuit to race. **Franchoek** has been a disappointment this season, losing his way badly on his last 2 starts; he'll reportedly go chasing next season, though does lack size and isn't an obvious one to excel in that sphere. **Othermix** ran as if having a problem, one of the first beaten and pulled up in the straight.

- **LIVE COMMENTARIES**
- **EXPERT ANALYSIS**
- **KEY INTERVIEWS**

Listen at timeform.com/radio
Find the daily podcasts at iTunes

TIMEFORM.COM
Opinion & analysis at your fingertips

HOMEPAGE

Free articles and features include:

Timeform's View, Essay of the Week and Race of the Day.

Your gateway to the Timeform Shop and Downloads...

RACE CARDS

Published for every meeting in Britain & Ireland

- Adjusted Ratings & Commentaries–for every runner in every race
- Ratings summary–instant form insight for every horse
- Horses In Focus highlighted

Download for just £5 at timeform.com

RACE PASSES

Daily (£10), 7-day (£25), and 28-day (£60) subscriptions give open access to the Timeform database for every race for as long as you need.

- A single race with adjusted Timeform ratings
- In-Play symbols
- Latest Betfair prices
- **Horse Search for every runner >>>>>>**

View a free sample Race Pass daily on the timeform.com homepage

also available individually £1.50 each

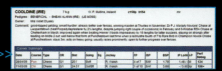

also available separately – 'a racing CV for 50p'

THE HOME OF WINNERS SINCE 1948

Timeform's 'Top Hundred'

	Hurdlers
174+	Big Buck's
171	Punchestowns
166	Binocular
166	Kasbah Bliss
166	Mighty Man
164	Celestial Halo
164	Punjabi
164	Solwhit
163	Fiveforthree
161	Crack Away Jack
161	Lough Derg
160	Sizing Europe
159	Muirhead
158	Fair Along
158	Katchit
158	Sublimity
157p	Hurricane Fly
156	Catch Me
156d	Hardy Eustace
156	Jazz Messenger
156	Powerstation
156	Quevega
155p	Mikael d'Haguenet
155	Blue Bajan
155	Brave Inca
155	Pettifour
154	Al Eile
154	Osana
154	Sentry Duty
154	Tazbar
154	Won In The Dark
153§	Harchibald
153	Coolcashin
153	Jered
152	Duc de Regniere
152	Pandorama
151	Aitmatov
151	Ashkazar
151	Essex
151	Mobaasher
151	Snap Tie
151	Weapon's Amnesty
150p	Karabak
150§	Clopf
150	Ninetieth Minute
150	United
150	Whatuthink
149§	Afsoun
149	Alpha Ridge
149	Blazing Bailey
149	Pierrot Lunaire
149	Shakervilz
148	American Trilogy
148	Ebaziyan
148	Hora
148	Made In Taipan
148	Pride of Dulcote
148	Sporazene
148	The Polomoche
147	Andytown
147	Cape Tribulation
147	Diamond Harry
147	Go Native
147	Katies Tuitor
147	P'tit Fute
146p	Bensalem
146p	Woolcombe Folly
146	China Rock
146	Inchidaly Rock
146	Souffleur
146	Straw Bear
146	Whiteoak
145+	Definity
145+	Mad Max
145	Aigle d'Or
145	Ballydub
145	Chomba Womba
145	Copper Bleu
145	Dave's Dream
145	Kazal
145	Medermit
145	Nicanor
145	River Liane
145	Serabad
145	Songe
145	The Midnight Club
145	Time For Rupert
144+	Cousin Vinny
144x	No Refuge
144	Beau Michael
144	Five Dream
144	Group Captain
144	Hills of Aran
144	Pennek
143p	Big Zeb
143p	Sports Line
143p	Sunnyhillboy
143	Comhla Ri Coig
143	Franchoek
143	Kayf Aramis
143	Knockara Beau
143	Ogee
143	One Gulp
	Chasers
184	Kauto Star
179	Master Minded
171+	Denman
170	Madison Du Berlais
170	Voy Por Ustedes
169	Exotic Dancer
168	Neptune Collonges
167+	Well Chief
167	Notre Pere
166§	Albertas Run
166	Joe Lively
165	Halcon Genelardais
165	Imperial Commander
165	Noland
165d	Star de Mohaison
164§	Tidal Bay
164	Big Zeb
164	The Listener
163	Schindlers Hunt
162+	Big Buck's
162§	Ollie Magern
162	Cloudy Lane
162	My Will
162	Nacarat
162	Roll Along
161	Air Force One
161	Snoopy Loopy
161	Tamarinbleu
159	Jack The Giant
159	Mister Top Notch
159	Mon Mome
158p	Cooldine
158	Mansony
158	Twist Magic
157	Comply Or Die
157	Nozic
157	Thyne Again
157	War of Attrition
156	Barker
156	Black Apalachi
156	Glenfinn Captain
156	Gone To Lunch
156	Monet's Garden
156	Petit Robin
156	Scotsirish
155	Barbers Shop
155	Forpadydeplasterer
155	Gungadu
154	Briareus
154	Garde Champetre
154	Gwanako
154	Kalahari King
154	Miko de Beauchene
154	Monkerhostin

Rating	Horse
154	Watson Lake
153§	Mr Pointment
153	Carthalawn
153	Dbest
153	Newmill
153	Oslot
153	Something Wells
153	State of Play
152§	Ashley Brook
152	Dear Villez
152	Tartak
151+	Big Fella Thanks
151	Mister McGoldrick
151	Snowy Morning
150p	Atouchbetweenacara
150p	Tricky Trickster
150x	Knowhere
150x	Lord Henry
150	Chapoturgeon
150	Rambling Minster
150	Stan
150	Trafford Lad
149+	Rare Bob
149x	Turko
149§	Opera Mundi
149	Carruthers
149	Conna Castle
149	I'msingingtheblues
149	Irish Invader
149	L'Ami
149	Natal
149	One Cool Cookie
148p	Joncol
148x	Cailin Alainn
148§	Darkness
148	Breedsbreeze
148	Character Building
148	Chelsea Harbour
148	Don't Push It
148	Ornais
148	Slim Pickings
148	Takeroc
148	Vic Venturi
147p	Aran Concerto
147?	Our Vic
147x	Ungaro
147§	Il Duce
147§	Moon Over Miami
147	J'Y Vole
147	Mahogany Blaze
147	Money Trix
147	Niche Market
147	Oh Crick
147	Pablo du Charmil
147	Parsons Legacy
147	Perce Rock
147	Planet of Sound
147	Possol
147	Royal County Star
147	Wichita Lineman
Juvenile Hurdlers	
155p	Zaynar
154	Walkon
147	Jumbo Rio
146	Mourad
145p	Ebadiyan
145	Trenchant
144	Mr Thriller
142	Starluck
141p	Bouggler
141	Ski Sunday
139+	Tasheba
138	Reve de Sivola
137	Master of Arts
137	Saticon
137	Silk Hall
137	Tharawaat
135	Hebridean
134	Alexander Severus
133	Indian Groom
133	Silk Affair
Novice Hurdlers	
157p	Hurricane Fly
155p	Mikael d'Haguenet
152	Pandorama
151	Weapon's Amnesty
150p	Karabak
149	Alpha Ridge
148	American Triology
148	Pride of Dulcote
147	Cape Tribulation
147	Diamond Harry
147	Go Native
146p	Bensalem
146	China Rock
146	Inchidaly Rock
145+	Definity
145+	Mad Max
145	Copper Bleu
145	Medermit
145	The Midnight Club
145	Time For Rupert
Novice Chasers	
158p	Cooldine
156	Barker
156	Gone To Lunch
155	Forpadydeplasterer
154	Kalahari King
152	Tartak
151+	Big Fella Thanks
150p	Tricky Trickster
150	Chapoturgeon
150	Trafford Lad
149+	Rare Bob
149	Carruthers
149	I'msingingtheblues
148p	Joncol
148	Breedsbreeze
147p	Aran Concerto
147	Niche Market
147	Oh Crick
147	Planet of Sound
147	Wichita Lineman
National Hunt Flat Horses	
131	Dunguib
120	Luska Lad
119	Some Present
118	Rite of Passage
118	Sitting Tennant
117	Frascati Park
116	Lidar
116	Pandorama
116	Qroktou
116	Quel Espirit
116	Sweeps Hill
116	Western Leader
115	Cadspeed
115	Candy Creek
115	City Theatre
115	Fionnegas
115	Shalone
115	Shinrock Paddy
115	Sicilian Secret
115	Uimhiraceathair
Hunter Chasers	
139p	Cappa Bleu
135*	Oracle des Mottes
134	Limerick Boy
134	Trust Fund
131	Christy Beamish
130	Agus A Vic
130§*	Kaldouas
130	Turthen
129	Baby Run
128p	An Siorrac
128	Amicelli
127	Carronhills
127	Having A Cut
127*	McEvoy
126	Distant Thunder
126x	Take The Stand
124p	Simonsberg
124	Alvino
124d*	Even More
123+	Always Right

Racecourse Characteristics

The following A-Z guide covers all racecourses in England, Scotland and Wales that stage racing over the Jumps. A thumbnail sketch is provided of each racecourse's characteristics .

AINTREE

The Grand National course is triangular with its apex (at the Canal Turn) the furthest point from the stands. It covers two and a quarter miles and is perfectly flat throughout. Inside is the easier Mildmay course, providing a circuit of one and a half miles, which has birch fences. A major feature of the Mildmay course is its sharpness; the fences there are appreciably stiffer than used to be the case. The Grand National is run over two complete circuits taking in sixteen spruce fences first time round and fourteen the second, and, in spite of modifications to the fences in recent years, the race still provides one of the toughest tests ever devised for horse and rider. The run from the final fence to the winning post is 494 yards long and includes an elbow.

ASCOT

The triangular, right-handed circuit is approximately a mile and three quarters round; the turns are easy and the course is galloping in nature. The sides of the triangle away from the stands have four fences each, and the circuit is completed by two plain fences in the straight of two furlongs. After being closed for two seasons due to major redevelopment work, NH racing returned to Ascot in 2006/7. The fences are still stiff, though improved drainage means conditions don't get so testing as they once did.

AYR

The Ayr course is a left-handed circuit of one and a half miles comprising nine fences, with well-graduated turns. There is a steady downhill run to the home turn and a gentle rise to the finish. There is a run-in of 210 yards. When the going is firm the course is sharp, but conditions regularly get extremely gruelling, making for a thorough test.

BANGOR-ON-DEE

Bangor has a left-handed circuit of approximately one and a half miles. It's a fair test of jumping, with nine fences in a circuit, and the run-in is about a furlong. The track is fairly sharp because of its many bends, the paddock bend being especially tight.

CARLISLE

The course is right-handed, pear-shaped and undulating, a mile and five furlongs in extent. The track is a particularly stiff one and the uphill home stretch is very severe. There are nine fences to a circuit with a run-in of 300 yards. Perhaps due to the nature of the track, the fences are among the easiest in the country. A long-striding galloper suited by a real test of stamina is an ideal type for Carlisle.

CARTMEL

This tight, undulating, left-handed circuit is a little over a mile round. There are six fences to a circuit and the winning post is a little over a furlong from the turn into the finishing straight, which divides the course and which the horses enter after two circuits for races over seventeen furlongs or three circuits for three and a quarter miles. The fences are tricky, with four coming in quick succession in the back straight; the run of half a mile from the last fence is the longest in the country.

CATTERICK BRIDGE

The Catterick course is a left-handed, oval-shaped circuit of around a mile and a quarter, with eight fences and a run-in of about 280 yards. Races over two miles and three miles one and a half furlongs start on an extension to the straight and over two miles the first fence is jumped before joining the round course. Catterick's undulations and sharp turns make it unsuitable for the long-striding galloper and ideal for the nippy, front-running type.

CHELTENHAM

There are two left-handed courses at Cheltenham, the Old Course and the New Course. The Old Course is oval in shape and about one and a half miles in extent. There are nine fences to a circuit, only one of which is jumped in the final straight.

The New Course leaves the old track at the furthest point from the stands and runs parallel to it before rejoining at the entrance to the finishing straight. This circuit is a little longer than the Old Course and has ten fences, two of which are jumped in the final straight.

The most telling feature of the Old and the New Courses is their testing nature. The fences are stiff and the last half mile is uphill, with a run-in of just over a furlong. The hurdle races over the two tracks are quite different in complexion, with only two flights jumped in the final 6f on the New Course. The four-mile and two-and-a-half-mile starts are on an extension, with five fences, which bisects both courses almost at right angles. The two-mile start is also on this extension, and two fences are jumped before reaching the main circuit.

There is also a cross-country course at Cheltenham, laid out in the centre of the conventional tracks.

CHEPSTOW

Chepstow is a left-handed, undulating, oval course, nearly two miles round with eleven fences to a circuit, a five-furlong home straight, and a run-in of 250 yards. Conditions can be very testing. With five fences in the straight, the first part of which is downhill, front runners do well here.

DONCASTER

The Doncaster course is a left-handed pear-shaped circuit of approximately two miles, and has eleven fences—including four in the home straight—with a run-in of 240 yards. Only one fence is jumped twice in races over two miles. The course is flat apart from one slight hill about one and a quarter miles from the finish. The track is well drained and often produces conditions which naturally favour horses with more speed than stamina.

EXETER

This is a hilly course, galloping in nature. Conditions can get extremely testing in midwinter and the exact opposite in drier periods, the course being without an artificial watering system. Its right-handed two-mile circuit is laid out in a long oval, with eleven fences and a run-in of around 170 yards. The chase course is on the outside of the hurdles one, but the inside track is often used on the home turn regardless of whether the races are over fences or not. The half-mile home straight is on the rise all the way to the finish.

FAKENHAM

Fakenham is an undulating, very sharp track, ideal for the handy, front-running type and unsuitable for the long-striding animal. The left-handed, square-shaped track has a circuit of a mile and a run-in of 250 yards. There are six fences to a circuit and, probably on account of most races being well run, the course takes more jumping than most which cater for horses of lesser ability.

FFOS LAS

The wide, galloping, left-handed circuit of 1½ miles, with a straight of just over 4f. It has no undulations but a very slight rise over the course of the back straight and the opposite in the home straight. There are short run-ins for both hurdles and chases. Early indications are that it is a very fair track, though there has been a tendency at the first few meetings for the races to be steadily run, meaning the fields haven't got stretched and large numbers of runners have still been in contention turning for home.

FOLKESTONE

The course is right-handed and approximately eleven furlongs round. The turns are easy, but the undulations can put a long-striding horse off balance. There are seven fences to a circuit, which are relatively easy, and the run-in is about a furlong.

FONTWELL PARK

There are two types of track at Fontwell, the hurdle course being left-handed, an oval about a mile in circumference with four flights, and the chase course a figure of eight with six fences which are all in the two straight intersections linked with the hurdle course. Fontwell is not a course for the big, long-striding horse, and it can cause problems for inexperienced chasers.

HAYDOCK PARK

The 2007/8 season was the first since redevelopment work at Haydock resulted in a resiting of the chase course. All jump races are now run on the old hurdle course, using portable fences instead of the traditional ones, some of which had a slight drop on landing. There are four fences (instead of five) in the back straight, with the open ditch now the second there instead of the last, whilst there are still four fences and a water jump in the home straight. The 440-yard run-in is no more, however, it's length significantly reduced as only the water jump is omitted on the final circuit. The new chase course has a tighter configuration than the old one and doesn't test jumping to the same extent.

HEREFORD

Hereford's right-handed circuit of about a mile and a half is almost square and has nine fences, of which the first after the winning post has to be taken on a turn. The home turn, which is on falling ground, is pretty sharp but the other bends are easy.

HEXHAM

Hexham has an undulating left-handed circuit of a mile and a half with ten fences. Although the fences are easy the course is very testing; the long back straight runs steeply downhill for most of the way but there is a steep climb from the end of the back straight to the home straight, which levels out in front of the stands. The finish is on a spur, which has one fence and a run-in of a furlong.

HUNTINGDON

The course is right-handed, oval with easy bends, and is a flat, fast track about one and a half miles in length. There are nine fences to a circuit, some of them rather tricky, and the water jump was filled in during summer 2008, astroturf replacing the water. Huntingdon favours horses with speed over stamina, sluggards seen to best advantage only under extremely testing conditions.

KELSO

The left-handed Kelso course has two tracks, the oval hurdle course of approximately a mile and a quarter and the chase course of approximately eleven furlongs. There are nine fences to be jumped in a complete circuit of the chase course; the last two aren't jumped on the final circuit and the first open ditch isn't taken at the start of the chases over four miles. The run-in, which is on an elbow, is a tiring one of 440 yards. The hurdle track is tight, with a particularly sharp bend after the stands.

KEMPTON PARK

Kempton is a very fair test for a jumper; it is a flat, triangular circuit of one mile five furlongs and is right handed. There are nine fences to a circuit, three of them in the home straight, and although they are quite stiff they present few problems to a sound jumper. After the laying of an all-weather course, which necessitated the removal of the water jump, NH racing returned in 2006/7.

LEICESTER

The right-handed course is rectangular in shape, a mile and three quarters in extent and has ten fences. Leicester is a stiff test and the last three furlongs are uphill. The run-in of 250 yards has a slight elbow on the chase course 150 yards from the winning post. Races over hurdles are run on the Flat course and the going tends to be a good deal more testing than over fences.

LINGFIELD PARK

Lingfield is about a mile and a half in length, triangular and taken left-handed, sharp, has several gradients and a tight downhill turn into the straight. Nine relatively easy fences are jumped on a complete circuit. Bumper races are now usually run on the all-weather track.

LUDLOW

Ludlow is a sharp, right-handed, oval track, with a nine-fence chase circuit about a mile and a half and a run-in of 250 yards. The fences are easy. The hurdle course, which runs on the outside of the chase course, has easier turns. Whereas the chase course is flat, the hurdle course has slight undulations but they rarely provide difficulties for a long-striding horse.

MARKET RASEN

There is a right-handed, oval circuit of a mile and a quarter, seven relatively easy fences and a run-in of 250 yards at Market Rasen. The track is sharp, covered with minor undulations, and favours the handy, nippy type of horse.

MUSSELBURGH

A right-handed oval track a little over a mile and a quarter in extent, almost flat with sharp bends, favouring the handy type of animal and also front runners. There are eight fences (four in each straight) or six flights of hurdles (three in each straight nowadays) to a circuit. The two-mile start is on a spur on the last bend.

NEWBURY

The oval Newbury course, with eleven fences to the circuit, is about a mile and three quarters in circumference and is set inside the Flat track, following a left-handed line. It is one of the fairest courses in the country, favouring no particular type of horse. The home straight is five furlongs with three plain fences, an open ditch (the water jump being omitted on the final circuit) and a run-in of 255 yards. There are seven hurdles to a circuit, four in the back straight and three in the home straight with a long run to the third last. The course is galloping in nature, with easy bends, plenty of room and few significant undulations.

NEWCASTLE

The jumps track is laid out inside the Flat course, its left-handed circuit of one and three quarter miles containing ten fences. There is a steady rise from the fifth last to the winning post and the course puts a premium on stamina, with the fences being on the stiff side. The ground is often testing here, too.

NEWTON ABBOT

Newton Abbot has a flat, oval, tight, left-handed circuit of about nine furlongs that favours the handy sort of horse. There are seven relatively easy fences to a circuit, and a very short run-in. The nineteen-furlong start over hurdles is on a spur after the winning post and the first hurdle is jumped only once.

PERTH

Perth is a right-handed circuit of one and a quarter miles, with eight fences to the circuit. The course has sweeping turns and quite a flat running surface. The water jump is in front of the stands and is left out on the run-in, leaving a long run from the last fence to the winning post.

PLUMPTON

The oblong-shaped course is only nine furlongs in circumference and has tight, left-handed bends, steep undulations, and an uphill home straight. The climb becomes pretty steep near the finish but the course is not a particularly stiff one; it favours the handy and quick-jumping types. There are six fences to a circuit and the run-in is 200 yards.

SANDOWN PARK

Sandown is a right-handed, oval-shaped course of thirteen furlongs, with a straight run-in of four furlongs. There is a separate straight course which runs across the main circuit over which all five-furlong races are decided. From the mile-and-a-quarter starting gate, the Eclipse Stakes course, the track is level to the turn into the straight, from there it is uphill until less than a furlong from the winning post, the last hundred yards being more or less level. The five-furlong track is perfectly straight and rises steadily throughout. Apart from the minor gradients between the main winning post and the mile-and-a-quarter starting gate, there are no undulations to throw a long-striding horse off balance, and all races over the round course are very much against the collar from the turn into the straight. The course is, in fact, a fairly testing one, and over all distances the ability to see the trip out well is important.

SEDGEFIELD

The circuit is approximately a mile and a quarter, oval, and taken left-handed. It is essentially sharp in character and the eight fences are fairly easy, though some uphill sections of the undulating ground, notably the final 150 yards, are punishing. The run-in is 200 yards.

SOUTHWELL

The Southwell track is laid out in a fairly tight, level oval of less than a mile and a quarter. In 2002/3 the circuit was divided into a summer and a winter track, with the slightly larger summer track on the outside of the winter one. The runners go left-handed. There are seven portable fences to a circuit which are stiff ones for a minor track. The brush-type hurdles can also catch out less fluent jumpers.

STRATFORD-ON-AVON

This sharp track is flat, triangular in shape and has a left-handed circuit of a mile and a quarter, taking in eight fences. One of the fences in the home straight was removed in the summer of 2007, but a water jump was introduced at the start of the following season just before the winning line and is obviously bypassed on the final circuit.

TAUNTON

The right-handed course is a long oval, about a mile and a quarter round, and has seven fences, four in the back straight and three in the home straight. The fences are easy enough but, due the the sharp nature of the track, catch out plenty more runners than might be expected. The bend after the winning post is tight and the chase run-in short.

TOWCESTER

Towcester is a right-handed course, a mile and three quarters round, and is the stiffest track in the country. The last mile or so is very punishing, with a steep climb to the home turn and a continuing rise past the winning post. Stamina is at a premium and conditions can get very testing. There are ten fences on the circuit, two (small obstacles) in the finishing straight, but they seldom present problems, with the exception of the two downhill ones running away from the stands. The run-in is 200 yards.

UTTOXETER

The course is an oval of approximately a mile and a quarter with a long, sweeping, left-handed bend into the straight and a sharper one after the winning post. The hurdle course in particular suits the handier type of horse. There are minor undulations and the back straight has slight bends. The ground can get extremely testing, so that few horses act on it. There are eight fences, with a run-in of around 170 yards. Races of two miles, three and a quarter miles and four and a half miles are started on a spur on the last bend.

WARWICK

Warwick's left-handed course is a mile and three quarters round with ten fences to a circuit. Five of them come close together in the back straight and sound jumping is at a premium. The bends are rather tight and the track is a sharp one, favouring the handy horse. There is a run-in of 250 yards.

WETHERBY

The course is left-handed, with easy turns and follows a long oval circuit of a mile and a half, during which nine fences are jumped, the four in the home straight now on the inside of the hurdles track. It provides a very fair test for any horse, but is ideal for the free-running, long-striding individual with plenty of jumping ability.

WINCANTON

Wincanton is a level course with an oval, right-handed circuit of around a mile and a half containing nine fences. It is essentially sharp in nature and, as such, provides a stiffish test with regards to jumping. The run from the last fence is only about 200 yards.

WORCESTER

The course is laid out in the shape of a long oval of thirteen furlongs, flat throughout with easy, left-handed turns. There are nine well-sited fences, five in the back straight, four in the home straight, and a run-in of 220 yards. Brush-type hurdles are used at Worcester and can cause jumping problems. Severe flooding in summer 2007 caused considerable damage to both the racing surface and stands.

WE'VE GOT IT COVERED

TIMEFORM RACE CARDS ARE AVAILABLE FOR EVERY MEETING EVERY DAY

£5 each at timeform.com
or call 01422 330540

THE HOME OF WINNERS SINCE 1948

Index

A

Abroad	111
Acordeon	5
Afsoun	115
Ainama	100
Air Force One	120
Al Eile	122
Alarazi	101
Albertas Run	119
Alderley Rover	5, 71
Alegralil	6, 71
Alph	105
Alpha Ridge	118
Andytown	7
Another Brother	76, 86
Apartman	86
Arctic Shadow	76
Art Sleuth	116
Ashkazar	105
Ashley Brook	109
Askthemaster	45
Atouchbetweenacara	8, 73, 91
Australia Day	9

B

Baily Storm	76
Bakbenscher	10, 65
Bally Sands	117
Ballydub	59
Ballyfitz	108
Barbers Shop	119
Benbane Head	111
Bensalem	11, 64
Big Buck's	90, 97, 113
Big Fella Thanks	92, 95
Big Zeb	109
Binocular	93, 96, 104
Blazing Bailey	63, 114
Blue Bajan	105, 122
Bohemian Lass	108
Brave Inca	105
Briareus	109
Bringbackthebiff	103
Browns Baily	117
Bygones of Brid	111

C

Cadspeed	111
Calgary Bay	102
Cape Tribulation	117
Cappa Bleu	92
Carole's Legacy	12
Carolina Lady	13
Carruthers	107
Casey Jones	107
Catch Me	122
Celestial Halo	103, 122
Cerium	120
Chariot Charger	118
Cheating Chance	102
Chilli Rose	14, 65
China Rock	106
Cloudy Lane	67
Cockney Trucker	14
Coin of The Realm	15
Comhla Ri Coig	68
Cool Operator	102
Cooldine	107
Copper Bleu	15, 100
Cornas	102
Cousin Vinny	100
Crack Away Jack	104
Cranky Corner	110
Cuckoo Pen	17

D

Danimix	76
Dechiper	17
Definity	18
Den of Iniquity	118
Denman	119
Devon Native	19
Diablo	118
Diamond Harry	106
Dorset Square	106
Double Dash	111
Drunken Sailor	45
Duc de Regniere	91
Dunguib	110

E

Ebadiyan	116
Ebaziyan	105
Ernst Blofeld	70
Etoile d'Or	86
Exotic Dancer	119
Express Leader	20

F

Fabalu	71
Fair Along	57, 114
Fennis Boy	111
Fiendish Flame	70
Fiveforthree	92, 121
Flintoff	74
Follow The Plan	102
Forpadydeplasterer	101
Franchoek	122
Frascati Park	21

G

Gagewell Flyer	111
Garleton	22
Gauvain	102
Glenwood Knight	22, 71
Gloucester	101
Go Native	99
Gobejolly	86
Golan Way	100
Golden Silver	103
Gone To Lunch	108
Gus Macrae	79
Gwanako	112

H

Halcon Genelardais	62, 120
Harchibald	105
Hardy Eustace	104, 122
Harry The Hawk	23
Henry King	111
Hills of Aran	122
Hold Em	108
Horner Woods	107
Hurricane Fly	93

I

I'msingingtheblues	102
Idle Talk	69
Imperial Commander	112
Intensifier	101
Isn't That Lucky	24

J

Jaffonnien	46
James de Vassy	24
Jamestown Bay	87
Jered	104, 122
Jessies Dream	47
Jumbo Rio	116
Junior	106
Just Rob	116

K

Kalahari Kinµg	101
Kangaroo Court	25, 101
Karabak	63, 105
Kasbah Bliss	113
Katchit	62, 104
Kauto Star	89, 118
Kempes	100
Keogh's Bar	81
Killyglen	91, 108
Knight Legend	113
Knockara Beau	106
Knowhere	120
Kornati Kid	60

L

L'Antartique	113
Lap of Honour	26
Latin America	111
Lead On	60
Lead The Parade	110
Leamington Lad	101
Lenabane	47

Leo's Lucky Star	100
Lethal Weapon	116
Lie Forrit	27
Lightening Rod	111
Lightning Strike	108
Little Shilling	75
Lodge Lane	108
Long Strand	111
Loosen My Load	48
Luska Lad	49

M

Mad Max	106
Madame Mado	28
Made In Taipan	101
Madison du Berlais	119
Mahogany Blaze	109
Maidstone Mixture	116
Manor Park	75
Marchand d'Argent	29
Marodima	109
Marsool	72
Mask of Darkness	49
Massini's Maguire	59, 107
Master Charm	86
Master Minded	90, 108
Master of Arts	116
Meath All Star	111
Medermit	64, 99
Micheal Flips	100
Midnight Sail	117
Mighty Man	114
Mikael d'Haguenet	92, 105
Miko de Beauchene	120
Miss Overdrive	29, 65
Mister McGoldrick	113
Mobaasher	114
Monet's Garden	112
Morning Supreme	110
Mourad	115
Muirhead	104
My Turn Now	83
My Will	119

N

Nacarat	91, 121
Natal	121
Nenuphar Collonges	64
Neptune Collonges	119
Newmill	109, 121
No Refuge	114

O

Oh Crick	64
On Raglan Road	117
On The Way Out	117
Original	103
Osana	104
Oscar Rebel	50
Othermix	105, 122
Our Vic	113
Overrule	30

P

Pandorama	51
Panjo Bere	102
Pepe Simo	110
Pesoto	52
Petit Robin	109, 121
Pettifour	114
Phoudamour	30
Picture In The Sky	118
Planet of Sound	59, 101
Pliny	31
Porta Vogie	87
Powerstation	113
Pride of Dulcote	117
Prince Taime	59
Punchestowns	113
Punjabi	103

Q

Qozak	32
Qroktou	33
Qualypso d'Allier	34
Quartetto	106
Quel Esprit	110
Quinola des Obeaux	111
Quwetwo	106

R

Realt Dubh	106
Red Harbour	111
Red Moloney	100
Reve de Sivola	34, 115
Richard The Third	107
Right Stuff	35
Ring Bo Ree	36
Ring The Boss	58
Rite of Passage	110
River Liane	105
Roll Along	119
Ruby Kew	65
Rupestrian	75
Ruthenoise	106

S

Santa's Son	109
Schindlers Hunt	112, 121
Scotsirish	109, 121
Sentry Duty	105
Shakervilz	114
Shamari	100
Shinrock Paddy	110
Shoreacres	100
Sicilian Secret	111
Siegemaster	108
Silk Drum	116
Simarian	116
Snap Tie	58, 104
Snoopy Loopy	120
Solwhit	121
Some Present	110
Somersby	37, 99
Son of Flicka	70
Sona Sasta	37
Spanish Conquest	60
Sports Line	53
Stan	74
Star de Mohaison	120
Starluck	115
Stow	116
Sublimity	105
Sweeps Hill	53

T

Taipan's Way	54
Takeroc	121
Tara Taylor	38
Tarablaze	59
Tartak	102
Tasheba	38
Tatenen	103
Tazbar	114
Tharawaat	116
The Jigsaw Man	40
The Market Man	108
The Midnight Club	117
The Nightingale	106
Thetwincamdrift	117
Thumbs Up	70
Tidal Bay	112, 121
Tilabay	55
Toby Belch	118
Topjeu	40
Torphichen	100
Touch of Irish	41
Trenchant	115
Tricky Trickster	85, 92, 95
Twist Magic	109
Tyrrells Wood	116

U

Unforgettable	75
United	122
Unnamed	60

V

Vamizi	42
Vino Griego	42
Voy Por Ustedes	61, 112, 120

W

Walkon	115
War of The World	75
Weapon's Amnesty	117
Well Chief	108
Western Charmer	118
What A Friend	107
Whatuthink	114
Whiteoak	68, 104
Will Be Done	69
Won In The Dark	104
Wymott	43, 71

Z

Zaynar	115